You Can Do It—Lose Weight, Look Better, Feel Younger, Accomplish More!

Dr. Milton Lieberthal dramatically demonstrates why you should lose weight, the penalties of overweight, the positive approach to weight reduction (the <u>do's</u> instead of <u>don'ts</u>—at last!)—

- dieting and diets—how to keep them lively and challenging
- exercise—how to get the exercise you need without expensive equipment
- maintenance—the habits you've learned will keep working for you

Happiness is only the beginning of your rewards. START TODAY, AND ENJOY YOUR HEALTHFUL TRIP TO *THE LIGHTER SIDE OF LIFE!*

The Lighter Side Of Life

by
Milton M. Lieberthal, M.D., F.A.C.P.

POCKET BOOKS

New York   London   Toronto   Sydney   Tokyo

This book is intended to be used as a guide in a program of prescribed weight reduction only with the concurrence of and supervision by your own physician.

POCKET BOOKS, a division of Simon & Schuster Inc.
1230 Avenue of the Americas, New York, NY 10020

ISBN: 0-671-45164-2

First Pocket Books printing July 1983
Second Pocket Books printing September 1983
Third Pocket Books printing November 1988
Fourth Pocket Books printing January 1989

Dedicated to my wife,

Naomi,

who, happily, has always
heeded the admonitions
contained in this volume

CONTENTS

Part Two

HOW TO EAT YOURSELF THINNER

Part Three

THE TRUTH ABOUT DIET PILLS

Part Four

MODIFYING YOUR MUSCLES

Part Five

BEHAVING YOURSELF AND LIKING IT

Part Six

THE SWEET SMELL OF SUCCESS

The
Lighter
Side
Of Life

FOREWORD

Lose Weight and Be Happy

The enormous number of books and pamphlets written by physicians, nutritionists, food faddists, and physical-fitness buffs on the subject of losing weight attests to the importance the subject has achieved among the health and welfare concerns of our nation. We all would like to be slim and beautiful. How is it, then, that not all of us are? Certainly, the answer does not lie in any lack of reducing methods.

What, then, is the answer? If we have good methods and willing subjects, why isn't success assured? Certainly, the rewards that come from losing weight are many.

First and foremost, there is Health. Because there are chronic disease states that occur more often among the overweight than among normal-weight persons, and because reduction in weight can sometimes relieve those diseases, Health is number one.

Second, there is improved Appearance. Clothes fit better, and unsightly bulges disappear. Don't sell *appearance* short.

Third is Physical Fitness. Appropriate exercise that is usually part of a weight-reduction program can tone muscles and improve heart function.

Next is Pride—pride in one's accomplishment, pride in the compliments one's fellows pay when they see the improvement that has taken place, pride in one's self-image.

And finally, there is the more Youthful "feel" to life made possible by all the other good things that have happened. When you look better, feel better, and can accomplish more, you feel younger.

Well, I don't mean to be cute about this, but if you put the first letters of Health, Appearance, Physical fitness, Pride, and Youthful "feel" together, you get the acronym HAPPY, which was my point in the first place.

So, lose weight and be *HAPPY!*

M.M.L.

Part One

THE WHYS
AND
WHEREFORES
OF
LOSING WEIGHT

I

Fat Isn't Fun and Games

I long ago discovered that the picture of the jolly, happy fat person is frequently a picture drawn in sand, easily washed away by the first little wave of adversity that rolls in. By and large, it is my impression that Santa Claus is about the only perennially happy rotund individual on this planet. I believe others share my impression that overweight is too serious a matter to laugh away, too important a matter to dismiss lightly.

Overweight is a disease. It has causes, symptoms and signs, complications and treatment. It can be mild, moderate, or severe. It can affect almost any human being. It interferes with the quality of life, both physically and psychologically. Successful treatment reduces the complications and restores health. If overweight isn't a disease, what is it?

Let's look at it from that point of view. Let's suppose you are overweight. What's the harm? Possibly none, you may be interested to know. If you're in the low-medical-risk group of overweight persons, those who are less than 20 percent over their ideal weight, you probably need, at the most, a program of gentle weight loss. But if you're in the increased-medical-risk group, or 20 to 90 percent overweight, you need more vigorous weight reduction. Some potentially serious diseases can be associated with overweight of that degree. Often these diseases are relieved when the excess weight is lost. If you're more than 100 percent overweight, you are in a dangerous situation and should have immediate attention. (A table of proper weights according to sex, age, and type of frame may be found on pages 106–07.)

How did you get the way you are? What is the cause of your disease? Probably several mechanisms operated in sequence. But, whatever they were, the bottom line is that more calories wound up in your body stored as fat than were released by the amount of energy you expended.

There may have been familial or cultural reasons that implanted habits of overeating quite early in your life. As time goes by, eating habits tend to remain the same, while the expenditure of energy decreases as physical activity lessens with age.

Finally, your overeating may have resulted from some psychologic reason that has substituted food for the satisfaction you might have had from greater success in some other aspect of life. Depression, anxiety, and a desire for attention are common states associated with excessive food intake.

But let's get one thing straight. Worrying about which of these factors operated in your case could be a waste of time and mental effort. What's done is done. Now you must look to tomorrow.

Let me note at this point that I believe a discussion of the physiologic mechanisms by which the food you eat is actually converted to fat and stored in the fat cells of your body is beyond the scope of this volume. Suffice it to say that the digestive process is qualitatively the same whether a person is obese or of normal weight. The same juices do the same things to the same foods. Only the quantities involved differ. You should consult standard books on the digestive process and nutrition if you wish specific information on the subject.

In the meantime, we can conclude that your overweight took a longer time to develop than you think. We can also anticipate that a properly conducted weight-reduction program will get rid of your excess weight, but there are a couple of things you should realize right up front. One is that you, the patient, have the greatest part to play in the success of the program. And the satisfaction you get from that success can more than make up for the past "failures" that might have precipitated your overeating and weight gain in the first place. You *can* do it! You *will* do it!

Secondly, you must be prepared to follow a weight-control program for a long, long time, possibly for the rest of your life. But don't let that discourage you. Chances are the follow-up program won't be as strict as the program you will have followed to get your weight down. And chances are it will be easier to follow when the time comes, because you will have developed good habits that will help prevent you from ever overeating again and help motivate you to maintain your improved appearance and health.

After all, significant overweight is more than just a passing aberration. As I've already said, it is a chronic disease that requires medical supervision, just as a chronic disease like diabetes requires medical surveillance and continual treatment. Fortunately, there are certain features of long-term weight-loss maintenance that distinguish it from the treatment of chronic disease. The weight-loss maintenance can be successful. The weight is lost, the "disease" goes away. Only the treatment remains. With a chronic disease, that may not be so. The disease may remain, as well as the treatment.

When all is said and done, you're a lot better off making management of your weight a permanent part of your life than you would be managing a chronic disease.

Take advantage of your good fortune.

II

You Definitely Should Lose Weight

THE NITTY-GRITTY

Since you are too heavy for your height and age, you *need* to lose weight for a number of reasons, and it will be very helpful if you *want* to lose weight, too. There is no magic to losing weight, and no fad diet that will take weight off and keep it off. There is no pill that will reduce you regardless of what you eat. It is very unlikely that your glands have anything to do with your overweight, although your physician is in the best position to make that judgment. The chances are your excess weight accumulated while you ate more than you needed to and exercised less than you should have. The time has come for you to do something about it.

Fortunately, there is a lot you can do about it. More than your appearance is at stake. Studies have shown that social frustration, job anxieties, and poor self-image are more common among the overweight than among people of normal weight. Even more important, there is a great deal of evidence that overweight may lead to certain chronic diseases, some of which may actually shorten one's life if allowed to progress unchecked. The good news is that losing weight may reverse some of the problems associated with overweight.

A successful weight-reduction regimen usually includes:

- Reduction in dietary intake of calories, and often of other food factors, such as salt
- Behavior modification
- Appropriate exercise
- Possibly, the short-term use of medication to help control your appetite.

MYTHS* AND MONDAY MORNINGS

Before embarking on a weight-reduction program, you must become familiar with the truths about diet, medication, behavior modification, and exercise. That knowledge will help you follow the program prescribed for you. It will also help you to ignore the advice of well-meaning but uninformed relatives and friends who may urge you to "forget your diet" and eat some high-calorie food just to be sociable.

The first step in learning the truths is to get rid of the myths, of which there are a great many associated with reducing. Let me debunk the most common myths right here and now.

About Diet

MYTH: The ideal time to start on your diet is Monday morning.

---

*Myth: An ill-founded belief or imaginary story.

CORRECTION: Nonsense! The ideal time to start on your diet is right now, as soon as you've gotten your diet prescription.

MYTH: Starving is the best way to lose weight.

CORRECTION: Starving can have unfavorable effects on kidney and liver functions and, when carried to extremes, can change the chemical balance in the blood. People who lose weight by starving themselves are more apt to regain it. It is better to learn how to modify your eating habits so they stand you in good stead over the long haul.

MYTH: Alcoholic beverages do not put weight on.

CORRECTION: Alcohol is high in calories and does put weight on. Moreover, alcohol often stimulates the appetite, which only leads to the ingestion of even more calories.

MYTH: Calories do not count.

CORRECTION: They do count, and your present excess weight results from eating more calories than you have used up in your output of energy.

MYTH: A balanced diet is not necessary if one takes a vitamin/mineral capsule every day.

CORRECTION: A balanced diet of protein, carbohydrate, and fat is always necessary for good health. Such a diet usually contains the vitamins and minerals necessary for proper nutrition. However, your doctor may prescribe vitamin and mineral supplements anyway.

MYTH: You get fatter as you get older, regardless of what you eat.

CORRECTION: Not true. You may burn up less energy when you get older because physical activity and metabolism may decrease, but overweight is always the result of ingesting more food than the body needs.

MYTH: Water intake should be restricted during dieting.

CORRECTION: On the contrary, about six glasses of water between meals should be included daily.

About Diet Pills

MYTH: A "diet pill" makes you lose weight.

CORRECTION: Diet pills only suppress appetite. They may help you to eat less. Accordingly, they may be especially useful during the early weeks of a weight-reduction program to help reinforce the physician's dietary counsel (see Chapter IX).

About Behavior Modification

MYTH: It does not do any good to lose weight. You gain it all back sooner or later.

CORRECTION: It may take continued effort to keep the weight off, it's true, but the effort is well worthwhile, particularly if reversal of a disease process takes place as a result of the weight loss.

MYTH: The best way to lose weight is to get a good reducing-diet menu and follow it beginning Monday morning whenever you find you're gaining weight.

CORRECTION: The best way is to learn how to handle the situations in life that led to your overeating in the first place, such as weekend cocktail and dinner parties or anytime emotional upsets, so your weight control *never* gets away from you.

MYTH: To keep weight under control, it is necessary to diet for the rest of one's life.

CORRECTION: We all "diet," so to speak, but some diets contain too much food. If we can learn to think of what we can eat, and what goodies can be occasionally substituted without increasing the total caloric intake, dieting loses its "don't eat" character and assumes a much more pleasant, positive aspect.

About Exercise

MYTH: Exercising is more trouble than it's worth for reducing weight.

CORRECTION: Exercise speeds up the metabolism and counteracts the lowered basal metabolism often present when dieting is stopped. In the latter case, even normal eating may cause weight gain. Exercise is well worth the trouble.

MYTH: A hard workout causes more weight loss than milder activity.

CORRECTION: Exercise as part of a weight-reduction program should be done in a gradual, relaxed, nonpressured way. The temporary weight loss from sweating during hard exercise should not be confused with the true weight loss that results from a properly controlled, complete weight-loss program.

MYTH: Exercise by itself causes enough weight loss.

CORRECTION: Although exercise increases use of calories, it takes a great deal of exercise to cause weight loss without diet restriction as part of the program. As part of a weight-reduction program, exercise has a beneficial effect on the heart and lungs, the circulation, and muscles in general as well as increasing use of energy (calories). See page 69 for a table of the calories expended during various types of physical activity.

THE BOTTOM LINE

Overweight is associated with a number of chronic diseases. This association is particularly close if the excess weight consists mostly of fat, rather than muscle, which it does in everyone except the highly trained athlete. While appearance is often an important reason for losing weight, matters of health are even more important in your doctor's thinking. They should be important to you, too, and deserve some special discussion at this point.

Overweight and Disease

It has now been shown that the incidence of certain diseases is significantly higher among overweight persons than among those of normal weight. It is not hard to understand why gross overweight can be associated with damage to weight-bearing joints, such as the knees, and with joint strain, as in the lower back. After all, carrying around thirty, forty, or more extra pounds day after day presents the kind of mechanical disadvantage to muscles, ligaments, and joints we can all understand. It is not so obvious, however, that overweight of even lesser degree can be associated with some chronic diseases that may eventually threaten life if allowed to remain unchecked. Here's just a partial list:

HYPERTENSION: The relationship between overweight and high blood pressure is clear at every stage of adult life. Published findings from a screening of more than one million people revealed that persons who considered themselves overweight had prevalence rates of high blood pressure that were 50 percent to 300 percent higher than those with lower weights.

The good news is that a significant number of overweight individuals with high blood pressure could be brought to and maintained in blood-pressure remission by dietary management alone.

DIABETES: In one well-known clinic specializing in diabetes, it has been observed that more than 80 percent of newly diagnosed diabetics are overweight.

The good news is that diabetes that first appears in mid-adult life may often be satisfactorily controlled by diet alone, and the bad effects of obesity in this type of diabetes can be lessened by weight loss.

HEART DISEASE: Life assurance data have shown that, among the obese with no other impairment, deaths from cardiovascular and kidney diseases were 50 percent more than those expected on the basis of normal mortality.

The good news is that U.S. data covering overweight persons who subsequently reduced to normal weight showed a strong association with lower mortality.

OTHER DISEASES: Overweight has been shown to be responsible for the increased incidence of a number of other diseases that may be painful or responsible for considerable disability.

The good news is that these diseases, too, may improve or even disappear with reduction in weight.

If those facts aren't impressive enough, I have some more for you.

Overweight and Mortality

The relationship between significant overweight and the occurrence of disease does not stop simply with increased incidence of disease. It has also been shown that overweight is often associated with a *shortened life-span*. Further, when you regain your normal weight, you give yourself a better chance of living longer. That's not just gossip. Table 1 illustrates the results of one study. Read it, and then make up your mind once and for all to lose your excess weight.

Table 1

INCREASED MORTALITY WITH RISE IN WEIGHT*

If you are above average weight by	Your chance of death compared to normal is	
	for men	for women
10%	11% higher	6% higher
20%	20% higher	10% higher
30%	33% higher	25% higher
40%	50% higher	36% higher
50%	71% higher	Too few cases for analysis

Adapted from the 1979 *Build and Blood Pressure Study*. Society of Actuaries and the Association of Life Insurance Medical Directors of America.

Why would anyone who has a good chance to prolong life pass it by?

*For insured men and women.

III

Your New Creed

THE POSITIVE APPROACH TO WEIGHT REDUCTION

Too often, a program designed to change one's life-style, which is what weight reduction really is, tends to emphasize the things one should not do: "*Don't* eat fatty foods." "*Don't* eat desserts." *Don't* do this, *don't* do that. But those rules create negative thoughts and are really against the basic philosophy of our entire society. We are a nation of doers and movers. "*Do* unto others as you would have them do unto you." "*Honor* thy father and mother." "I *pledge* allegiance . . ." The thoughts behind those statements are all positive. And why not? If you wanted to learn to play tennis, you wouldn't think of it as a series of "don'ts." You would *hold* the racquet this way. *Strike* the ball that way. *Stand* here. *Run* there. They are all *positive* actions you would repeat again and again until your muscles learned how to respond positively to the action of the game.

You must think of your weight-reduction program the same way—all positives, no negatives.

1. *Do* learn the facts about overweight.
2. *Do* learn the truth about diet, medication, behavior modification, and exercise.
3. *Do* remember the relationship between overweight and chronic disease and the health advantage that normal-weight persons possess.

4. *Do* recognize that it is possible to succeed in a weight-reduction effort.
5. *Do* make the commitment here and now to lose the amount of weight your doctor recommends and to keep it off.

The *positive* approach leads to *success, improved appearance*, and *better health*. The effort is well worth it.

IV

The Chapter You Shouldn't Read

(Or, If You Do, Don't Tell Your Doctor)

I don't want you to read this chapter, because I feel compelled to say some things about the business of losing weight that are not about you. Nevertheless, they could have considerable impact on the degree of success you have with your weight-reduction efforts. I really mean "considerable impact," because, although these things I have to say are not about you, they *are* about your doctor.

In the past, during a visit to your doctor's office for a medical reason, you may have heard your doctor say, "You know, you really should lose some weight," or words to that effect. Most likely, that's all you heard. You may even have been handed a reduced-calorie-diet printout with the advice to follow it. Chances are that ended the matter for the time being. And chances are you were secretly relieved that the good doctor didn't chastise you for your obesity, or shame you into admitting how fat you were. You were glad to escape with your self-image reasonably intact.

Well, don't think for one moment that your doctor was uncaring, unskilled, or unknowledgeable. On the contrary, today's doctor is well aware of the hazards of significant overweight and the medical rewards for properly controlled weight loss, and *your* doctor is undoubtedly no exception. The medical literature is replete with scientific discussions of the subject. What the medical literature is not replete with is reports of long-term success with weight-reduction programs. People who lose weight often don't seem to keep it off. According to recent reports, there is also a high attrition rate among commercial weight-reduction programs. And on top of all that, your doctor probably remembers the many patients who have been told to lose weight but who have failed to do so, even though they were given more to help them than just the kind of simple oral advice you apparently wound up with.

In other words, there is an aura of failure that often surrounds the whole subject of weight reduction. And doctors are people, in most ways just like other people. We tend to shy away from our failures just like the rest of you. It takes time to convince a patient to lose weight, to give instructions about behavior modification, to calculate a diet, to plan an appropriate schedule of exercise, and to keep tabs on all of it in a meaningful way. Many physicians won't take the time to do all that unless they are assured that the patient is serious—and I do mean serious—about losing weight. Patients with diseases they didn't bring on themselves, diseases that respond only to antibiotics, or chemicals, or surgical procedures, that can be measured objectively and cured or, at least, controlled, are apt to attract a doctor's attention first. For these very same reasons, treatment for drug addiction has largely left the doctor's office and migrated to clinics and self-help groups. The management of alcoholism has followed the same path. In both of those instances, as with weight reduction, it's difficult to motivate the patient to achieve success, and when the patient fails to respond, the doctor loses motivation, too. The ultimate result is a diminished effort by the individual doctor and a take-over by others, often nonprofessionals, who try to do what the doctor and patient together failed to do in the doctor's office.

Well, that's one side of the coin. Now you know the subtle influences that may have modified your doctor's behavior. And now that I've said everything I felt compelled to say, what good can come of it? What's the other side of the coin? How does any of this help you?

Maybe it won't, but I have a suggestion to make. If you've determined you're serious about losing weight, and hold firmly to that resolve, and find in this book the ingredients of a weight-loss program you can live with, you can go to your doctor well motivated. When you tell your doctor you're going to follow a program of calorie restriction, appropriate exercise, and behavior modification, your doctor will immediately recognize that you've taken the trouble to really learn *how* to lose weight. And when you ask your doctor about the appropriateness of weight loss to your particular medical status, when you ask him to write down on page 36 how many pounds you are to lose and how many calories you are to eat, and when you inquire about how much exercise to take and the type of supervision necessary, your doctor will immediately recognize how well motivated you are and respond to the *sweet smell of success*.

You will get attention! You will be set apart from the failures who preceded you! And if you succeed, as you *will* succeed if you've read this far, you will have made a doctor *friend* for life. You will be a doctor *success*. As a result, you will receive the highest accolade a doctor can bestow, the label "a really good patient and a terrific person."

What more can you ask?

Part Two

HOW TO EAT YOURSELF THINNER

V

Where You Are Now

The time has come to record your present state, the eating habits that must be changed, your present weight, and the weight loss you intend to achieve. It is worth going to a doctor at this point and taking time to watch the doctor carefully record this information on the following pages so you both can monitor your progress and, incidentally, enjoy your success.

YOUR DOCTOR'S DIET PRESCRIPTION

1. Record patient's weight here and on the weight-loss record on page 92 . . . . _____

2. Calculate patient's present caloric intake (15 × present weight in pounds) . . . . _____

3. Pick out the weight you consider ideal for patient's height, age, sex, and type of frame from your height-weight tables. (If you do not have those tables handy, you will find them on page 106–07 in the Appendix to this volume.)
Record that ideal weight here . . . . _____

4. Determine the number of pounds to be lost . . . . _____

5. Prescribe the new caloric intake to average *one* pound weight loss per week* (present caloric intake minus 600) . . . . . . _____
or
the new caloric intake to average *two* pounds weight loss per week* (present caloric intake minus 1200) . . . . _____
Choose the one you prefer and also record it on page 38.

6. Calculate the number of weeks necessary to lose the excess weight . . . . _____

Starting Date_____ 19__
      (Mo.)   (Day)

(See the facing page for a sample Doctor's Diet Prescription.)

---

*On an average, weight loss will be much more rapid the first week or two—possibly three to four pounds with the minus-600 calorie intake, five to six pounds with the minus-1200 calorie intake. The weight loss becomes somewhat less rapid in subsequent weeks.

Your diet prescription should look something like this:

YOUR DOCTOR'S DIET PRESCRIPTION

1. Record patient's weight here and on the weight-loss record on page 92 .... **195 lbs**

2. Calculate patient's present caloric intake (15 × present weight in pounds) **2925**

3. Pick out the weight you consider ideal for patient's height, age, sex, and type of frame from your height-weight tables. (If you do not have these tables handy, you will find them on page 106–07 in the Appendix to this volume.) Record that ideal weight here **165**

4. Determine the number of pounds to be lost **30**

5. Prescribe the new caloric intake to average *one* pound weight loss per week* (present caloric intake minus 600)...... _____
   or
   the new caloric intake to average *two* pounds weight loss per week* (present caloric intake minus 1200) **1725**
   Choose the one you prefer and also record it on page 38.

6. Calculate the number of weeks necessary to lose the excess weight **15**

Starting Date __**JULY**__   __**5**__   19__**89**__
              (Mo.)   (Day)

---

*On an average, weight loss will be much more rapid the first week or two—possibly three to four pounds with the minus-600 calorie intake, five to six pounds with the minus-1200 calorie intake. The weight loss becomes somewhat less rapid in subsequent weeks.

VI

Where You Go from Here

Your weight-reduction program will include a well-balanced menu of foods to provide the correct number of calories per day, possibly the use of an appetite suppressant during the early weeks of your program, modification of your habits in certain respects, and a program of regular exercise. Each component of the total program is important. Together they accomplish the desired effect. Individually they are much less effective.

THE DIET FORMULA

Total number calories allowed per day (from page 36) .... ————

The first step is to pick out the number of portions in each food category in Table 2 that will provide a balanced diet and add up to the daily caloric allowance your doctor calculated for you (from page 36), as recorded above. In Table 2, in the left-hand column, find that daily calorie allowance and put a check mark next to the number of calories allowed. Read across on that line and then record in Table 3 the number of portions allowed for each food category to make up your prescribed calorie allowance.

Table 2

PICKING YOUR PORTIONS

Daily Calories Allowed	Fruit	Vegetables	Meat	Bread	Milk	Spreads
800	2	1	5	1	1½	0
900	3	3	5	1	1½	0
1000	3	3	5	1	2	0
1100	4	3	5	2	2	0
1200	4	3	5	3	2	1
1300	4	3	5	3	2	3
1400	3	3	6	4	2	3
1500	4	3	6	4	2	4
1600	4	3	6	5	2	5
1700	4	3	6	5	2½	5
1800	4	4	7	5	2½	5
1900	5	4	7	6	2½	5
2000	5	5	8	6	2½	5

When you have recorded on Table 3 the number of portions of each food category allowed in the formula for your balanced diet, you will have the key to the surprisingly extensive variety of foods you can eat and still lose weight. Refer to the pages indicated in the right-hand column of Table 3 to find all the choices available to you under each food category.

Be sure to ask your physician for any recommendations regarding the salt (sodium) content of your food. If there are restrictions, be sure to check the foods you choose against the column showing their salt content. A table showing foods with a high salt content appears on pages 117–18.

Table 3

PICKING YOUR FOODS

Food Category	Calories per Portion	Number Portions Allowed (fill in)	For Complete List, See Page
Fruit	40	_____	39
Vegetables	35–40	_____	39
Meat	75	_____	39
Bread	70	_____	39
Milk	170	_____	39
Spreads	45–50	_____	39
Unrestricted			
Vegetables	Negligible	As Desired	47–48
Beverages, certain	None	As Desired	48
Sweeteners, artificial	None	As Desired	49
Seasonings	None	As Desired	49
Relishes	None	As Desired	48
Soups	None	As Desired	48

Note: Your daily menu will consist of the number of portions of each food category specified, plus any amounts of any of the *un*restricted foods on pages 47–49 you care to add.

You may distribute these portions in the way most convenient to you on any given day. However, whenever possible, you should try to arrange your meals to be made up as follows:

Breakfast	Lunch	Dinner
Fruit juice	Salad or fruit	Juice
Egg, cereal, or bread	Egg, meat, or fish	Meat or fish
Spread	Vegetables	Vegetables
Beverage	Bread	Fruit
	Spread	Beverage
	Beverage	

Special Note: For those of you who find calorie counting impractical for one reason or another, I have included on pages 107–10 an already calculated 1000-calorie diet that can be followed, but only if your physician agrees that it's the appropriate diet for your condition.

VII

Eat, Drink, and Be Wary

You will find a table of Common Kitchen Measurement Equivalents on page 105 to help you distinguish a cup from a slice, a pat from a tbsp. Don't be bashful. Use it.

If your doctor sharply restricts the amount of salt (sodium) you may ingest, choose the foods with the lowest salt content, shown in the right-hand column of Table 4. Needless to say, you mustn't add salt at the table. Incidentally, home water softeners are said to add sodium to the water, so drinking or cooking with the water they produce should also be avoided. Be sure to read the labels of all packaged and canned goods for their salt content. Some food markets even contain a special section for low-sodium or sodium-free foods. But remember, get your doctor's advice on the matter of salt before embarking on a low-salt regimen.

And one other thing: you may find that some of the caloric values listed in this book differ somewhat from the values given for the same foods by other authors. Don't worry about it. The differences are usually small and not clinically important.

Note: All caloric values, sodium contents, and other constituents of foods and beverages are based mainly on data obtained from Bowes and Church's *Food Values of Portions Commonly Used*, 13th edition, revised by J. A. T. Pennington and H. N. Church (Philadelphia: J. B. Lippincott Company, 1980), reprinted with permission.

Table 4

FOODS BY CATEGORY

FRUITS—Number Portions Allowed . . . . _____
(fill in from list on page 39)
Each portion supplies approximately 40 calories, approximately 10 grams carbohydrate, and mostly a low sodium content.

		Salt Content per Portion (mg of sodium)†
Apple, raw, whole	1 small (2″ diam.)	1
Apple juice or cider	⅓ cup	1
Applesauce, canned, not sweetened	½ cup	2
Apricots, fresh	2 medium	1
Apricots, dried, uncooked	3 halves (large)	4
Avocado	¾ ounce	1
Banana, 6″ long	½	1
Berries (boysenberries, blackberries, blueberries, raspberries)	½ cup	1
Strawberries	10 large	—
Cantaloupe, 6″ diameter	¼	12
Cherries	10 large	2
Cherries, maraschino	5 large	—
Dates	2	1
Figs, fresh	1 large	1
Figs, dried	1 small	6
Fruit cocktail	½ cup	5
Grapefruit	½ small	1
Grapefruit juice	½ cup	1
Grapes	12	2
Grape juice	¼ cup	2
Honeydew melon, 5″ diameter	¼	12
Mandarin oranges	¼ cup	3.5
Mango	½ small	6
Nectarine	1 small	3
Olives, green, pickled	3	312
Orange, 2½″ diameter	1 small	1
Orange juice	½ cup	trace

		Salt Content per Portion (mg of sodium)
Papaya	¾ cup	4
Peach	1 medium	1
Pear	1 small	2
Pineapple, raw	¾ cup	1
Pineapple juice	⅓ cup	trace
Plums	2 medium	2
Prunes	2 medium	2
Prune juice	¼ cup	2
Raisins	2 tbsp.	6
Strawberries, raw	¾ cup	1
Tangerine	1 large	2
Watermelon	1 cup	2

†A dash — indicates salt content has not been calculated.

VEGETABLES—Number Portions Allowed ... _____
(fill in from list on page 39)
Each portion should consist of ½ cup. Each such portion supplies about 35–40 calories, 7 grams of carbohydrate, and 2 grams of protein. Vegetables should be cooked by steaming, preferably.

Beans, string (well filled)	147
Beets	196
Brussels sprouts	14
Carrots	200
Eggplant	3
Mushrooms (12 small or 5 large)	20
Onions (1 small)	8
Peas, green	160
Potato, white, boiled ½ medium (2¼″ diameter)	2
Pumpkin	1
Rutabaga	4
Scallions (5 small)	5
Squash, winter	1
Tomatoes	130
Turnips	40

(See Unrestricted on pages 47–49 for additional vegetables.)

MEAT, FISH, AND MEAT SUBSTITUTES—Number Portions
Allowed . . . . _____
(fill in from list on page 39)

Each portion supplies approximately 75 calories and 7 grams
of protein, 5 grams of fat. Meats should be boiled, broiled, or
roasted, *not* fried.

Salt Content
per Portion
(mg of sodium)†

MEAT AND POULTRY

		Salt Content
Lean beef	1 ounce	50
Lamb	(4″ × 2″ × ¼″)	35
Pork	″	270
Veal	″	30
Ham	″	20
Liver	″	36
Chicken	″	60
Turkey	″	33

COLD CUTS

Bologna	1 slice	292
Liverwurst	(4½″ × 2″ × ⅛″)	40
Luncheon meats	″	very high
Meat loaf	″	325

FISH AND SEAFOOD

Cod	1 ounce	25
Haddock	″	20
Mackerel	″	—
Trout	″	—
Clams	5 medium	36
Oysters	″	73
Scallops	″	175
Shrimp	″	120
Crab	¼ cup	—
Lobster	″	—
Salmon	″	—
Tuna	″	20
Sardines, canned in oil	2 medium	125

Salt Content
per Portion
(mg of sodium)†

CHEESE

Cheddar	¾ ounce	197
American	1 ounce slice (3½″ × 3½″ × ⅛″)	197
Swiss American	"	199
Cottage (not creamed)	¼ cup	225
EGG, soft or hard, poached or boiled	1 medium	60
PEANUT BUTTER	1 tbsp.	18
BACON, crisp	1½ med. slices	90

†A dash — indicates salt content has not been calculated.

BREAD AND CEREALS—Number Portions
Allowed . . . . ———
(fill in from list on page 39)
Each portion supplies approximately 70 calories, 15 grams of carbohydrate, 2 grams of protein.

Bagel	½	—
Biscuit, roll	1 (2″ diam.)	157
Bread, French, raisin (without icing), rye, white, whole-wheat	1 slice	128
Bread crumbs, dried	3 tbsp.	—
Bun (for hamburger or frankfurter)	½	250
Cornbread	1″ × 2″ × 2″	335
English muffin	½	100
Muffin	1 (2″ diam.)	160
Cake, angel or sponge, without icing	¾ ounce	42
Cereal, cooked	½ cup	
Cream of Wheat	"	1
Oatmeal	"	1
Wheatena	"	trace

Salt Content
per Portion
(mg of sodium)

Cereal dry (flakes or puffed)..	¼ cup	1
Cornstarch	2 tbsp.	—
Crackers, graham	2 (2½″ sq.)	94
Oyster	20 (½ cup)	290
Round	6	—
Rye wafer	3 (2″ × 3½″)	180
Saltine	6	198
Variety	5 small	—
Flour	2½ tbsp.	trace
Grits, cooked	½ cup	—
Matzah	1 (6″ diam.)	trace
Popcorn, popped, unbuttered, small-kernel	1½ cups	trace
Pretzels (3 ring)	6	324
Rice, cooked	½ cup	280
Spaghetti, macaroni, noodles, cooked	½ cup	1½
Special breads		
Hollywood, low calorie	2 slices	220
Melba, unsalted, toasted	5 slices	15
Pepperidge Farm	1 slice	140-180
Thomas' Protein Bread	1½ slice	—
Wonder Bread	1¼ slice	125
Zweiback	2 pieces	36
Tortilla, yellow or white corn..	1 (6″ diam.)	33

†A dash — indicates salt content has not been calculated.

MILK—Number Portions Allowed . . . . _____
(fill in from list on page 39)
Each portion supplies approximately 170 calories, 12 grams of carbohydrate, 8 grams of protein, 10 grams of fat.

MILK

Whole	1 cup	122
Skim (nonfat)	2 cups	244
Evaporated	½ cup	76
Powdered, whole	¼ cup	93

Salt Content
per Portion
(mg of sodium)

Nonfat dried milk powder .... ⅔ cup .... .205
Buttermilk .... 1 cup .... .212

SPREADS (AND FAT)—Number Portions
Allowed .... ————
(fill in from list on page 39)
Each portion supplies approximately 45–50 calories, 5 grams
of fat.

Butter .... 1 pat 41
Margarine .... 1 tsp. 49
Cream, half-and-half .... 3 tbsp. 18
   Heavy, 40% .... 1 tbsp. 6
   Light, 20% .... 2 tbsp. 12
   Sour .... 2 tbsp. 12
Cream cheese .... 1 tbsp. 35
Dressing, French .... 1 tbsp. .... .192
   Italian .... 1 tbsp. .... .290
   Mayonnaise .... 1 tsp. 42
   Mayonnaise-type .... 2 tsp. .... .100
   Roquefort .... 2 tsp. 70
Oil or cooking fat .... 1 tsp. .... .trace

UNRESTRICTED
For the most part, the following foods have little or no caloric
value when used in customary amounts. They may be taken
as desired to add more variety to any meal.

VEGETABLES—½ cup
Asparagus (6 spears) .... .271
Beet greens .... .130
Broccoli 15
Cabbage 20
Cauliflower 13
Celery 63
Chard 90
Cucumber 3
Dandelion greens 44

Salt Content
per Portion
(mg of sodium)†

Endive	14
Escarole	3
Lettuce	9
Parsley	15
Peppers	13
Pickles, sour, dill	high
and unsweetened	high
Pimientos	—
Radishes	18
Rhubarb	2
Sauerkraut	700
Spinach	71
Squash, summer	1
Turnip greens	—
Watercress	5

BEVERAGES
Coffee, black, no sugar	26
Coffee, instant	2
Postum, plain, no sugar	7
Tea, plain, no sugar	2
Carbonated water	30
Mineral water	—
Noncalorie, flavored and carbonated	27

RELISHES
Bread-and-butter pickles	168
Cucumber pickles	high
Dill pickles	high
Sour pickles	high

SOUPS
Bouillon	784
Clear soups without fat	high
Consommé	784

DESSERTS
Gelatin, flavored	8
Whipped topping, Cool Whip	1

Salt Content
per Portion
(mg of sodium)†

SEASONINGS

Celery seed	3
Chives for seasoning	—
Dill	trace
Horseradish	17
Lemon, juice, sections, or slices	1
Monosodium glutamate	750
	per tspnfl. (5 grams)
Mustard	63
Pepper	1
Salt (use very sparingly)	2132
	per tspnfl. (5 grams)

No-salt seasoning for eggs and meat
1 teaspoonful marjoram
1 teaspoonful savory
1 teaspoonful thyme
1/2 teaspoonful basil

Mix. Use to taste	trace
Sauces, prepared (such as Worcestershire, A-1)	50
Tabasco	22
Vinegar	trace
Garlic	1

SWEETENERS

Sugar substitutes (Adolph's, Sweet 'N Low)	20
Sugar Substitute (Sugar Twin)	6
Saccharin (1/4 grain tablet)	5
Saccharin (calcium salt)	0

†A dash — indicates salt content has not been calculated.

VIII

What You Always Knew About Booze, Burgers, and Butter Pecan but Ate Anyway

Man has, over the centuries, invented some striking ways of treating the grape, sugar cane, and chicken leg to make them taste better and better but, unfortunately, contain more calories. You should become familiar with the facts about those popular foods and beverages so you can regulate your intake appropriately.

ALCOHOLIC BEVERAGES

One drink a day, particularly for older adults, is sometimes permitted by doctors if allowance is made for the calories supplied by the drink and an appropriate amount of other food is omitted. No snacks should be taken with the drink. The caloric values of common drinks are listed in Table 5.

Table 5

CALORIC VALUES OF COMMON ALCOHOLIC DRINKS

		Calories
Brandy	30 ml. brandy glass	73
Crème de menthe	1 cordial glass	67
Highball		
(86 proof whiskey 1½ oz., ginger ale 8 oz.)		168
Dry martini	3½ oz.	140
Manhattan (sweet)	3½ oz.	164
Old-Fashioned	6 oz.	250
Tom Collins	10 oz.	180
Whiskey sour	1 cocktail	138
Bourbon ⎫		
Scotch ⎬	1½ oz.	105
Rye ⎭		
Beer	12 oz.	150
Beer, light	12 oz.	100
Ale	12 oz.	162
Wine		
Champagne, domestic	4 oz.	84
Sauterne, California	3½ oz.	84
Sherry, domestic	2 oz.	84

TEMPTATIONS

Many overweight persons have gotten that way by eating snacks or going on food binges that add many excess calories to the diet. The following list includes most of the common snacks and binge foods, and *all of them provide from 150 to 500 calories per ordinary portion*. No diet designed for a weight-reduction regimen includes such items. *Make up your mind to avoid them* like the plague.

Chocolate milk, plain or malted
Pastry, pie, layer cake
Cottage pudding
Sandwiches
Ice cream
Ice cream sundaes
Candy
Jellies and jams
Gravy
Sugar-coated cereals

FAST FOODS

If you are ever caught away from your usual haunts at mealtime and find your only choice is to eat at a fast-food emporium, let the calories listed in Table 6 be your guide. Just remember, if you feast today you may have to fast tomorrow!

Table 6

CALORIC VALUES OF FAST FOODS
(salt content provided where known)

	Calories	Salt Content per Portion (mg of sodium)
Arby's		
Junior Roast Beef	240	
Roast Beef	429	
Turkey Sandwich with dressing	402	
Super Roast Beef	705	
Arthur Treacher's Fish & Chips		
Fish, Chips, & Coleslaw:		
3-piece dinner	1100	
2-piece dinner	905	1000
Baskin Robbins		
One scoop with sugar cone:		
Chocolate Fudge	229	
French Vanilla	217	
Rocky Road	204	
Butter Pecan	195	
Chocolate Mint	189	
Jamoca	182	
Fresh Strawberry	168	
Mango Sherbet	132	
Burger King		
Whopper	630	
Whopper Junior	285	
Double Hamburger	325	
Hamburger	252	372
Cheeseburger	305	823
Hot Dog	291	
Whaler	744	

	Calories	Salt Content per Portion (mg of sodium)
French Fries	220	170
Vanilla Shake	331	306
Chicken Delight		
½ Chicken (4 pieces)	625	
Dairy Queen		
Small Dipped Cone	160	
Large Dipped Cone	450	
Small Sundae	170	
Large Sundae	400	
Small Malt	400	
Large Malt	830	
Hot Fudge Brownie Delight Sundae	580	
Banana Split	540	
Parfait	460	
Dilly Bar	240	
DQ Sandwich	190	
Dunkin' Donuts		
Plain Cake Donut	240	
Plain Honey Dipped	260	
Chocolate Honey Dipped	250	
Yeast-raised Donuts		
Sugared	255	
Honey Dipped	275	
(Add 50 calories for fillings)		
Hardee's		
Big Deluxe	600	
Fish Sandwich	275	
French Fries	240	
Chocolate Shake (8 oz.)	310	307
Hamburger	258	496
Huskie Deluxe	525	
Huskie Junior	475	
Howard Johnson's		
Small Cone	186	
Medium Cone	247	
Large Cone	370	
Sherbet	136	
7-oz. pkg. Fried Clams	357	

	Calories	Salt Content per Portion (mg of sodium)
Kentucky Fried Chicken		
One Drumstick	136	
3-piece special	660	
Dinner (chicken, mashed potatoes, gravy, coleslaw, roll)		
2-piece Original	595	
3-piece Original	830	
2-piece Crispy	665	
3-piece Crispy	950	
Long John Silver's		
Breaded oysters (6 pieces)	460	
Breaded clams (5 oz.)	465	
Chicken planks (4 pieces)	458	
Fish with batter (2 pieces)	318	
Treasure chest	467	
McDonald's		
Egg McMuffin	312	911
Hotcakes, Sausage, Syrup	507	
Hamburger	249	525
Double Hamburger	350	
Cheeseburger	309	724
Quarter Pounder	414	278
Quarter Pounder w/cheese	521	1206
Big Mac	557	963
Filet-O-Fish	406	707
French Fries	215	112
Hot Apple Pie	265	408
Chocolate Shake	317	329
Pizza Hut		
Thin and Crispy		
Cheese (1/2 of 10-in. pizza)	450	
Pepperoni (1/2 of 10-in. pizza)	430	
Thick 'n' Chewy		
Cheese (1/2 of 10-in. pizza)	560	
Pepperoni (1/2 of 10-in. pizza)	560	
Taco Bell		
Enchirito	454	
Beef burrito	466	

	Calories	Salt Content per Portion (mg of sodium)
White Castle		
Hamburger	164	
Cheeseburger	198	
French Fries	219	
Onion Rings	341	
Milk Shake	213	
Wendy's		
Cheeseburger	520	
Chocolate Shake	390	
Hamburger, double	630	

Part Three

THE TRUTH
ABOUT
DIET PILLS

IX

Of Pills, Potions, and Practitioners

Wise men have said, "Never say 'never.'" But if there's one admonition that comes as close to requiring the word *never* as any, it's "Never take medication as part of a weight-reduction program without first consulting a physician." Medicines are not always harmless. Medicines are not always helpful. You should depend on a professional to decide which is which in your case.

Having said that, I must now tell you about some of the medications some doctors do prescribe as part of a weight-reduction program. Although doctors who treat many overweight patients may possess great skill and considerable knowledge, they don't all agree about the proper medication to use, and I don't always agree with some of them who agree with each other. All that means is that the place pharmaceutical agents occupy in weight-reduction programs has not yet been carved in stone.

For instance, some physicians prescribe thyroid hormones in rather high doses because it has been shown that such hormones induce weight loss in some obese patients. However, thyroid hormones in high doses stimulate the metabolic rate, and that is not an innocuous procedure. The body burns up more calories than it needs to and weight may be lost, but damage to the heart and thyroid gland may result.

Some physicians prescribe diuretics, the so-called water pills, to increase fluid loss through the kidneys and bladder. Naturally, weight is lost whenever fluid is lost from the body, but it is really fat we want to lose, not water. Dehydration is not a desirable state, and weight loss on that basis is too temporary to be meaningful.

I have occasionally encountered a patient who is taking daily doses of a laxative with the idea of rushing food through the intestinal tract so fast that proper absorption can't take place and, presumably, weight will be lost as a result. I'm not sure many doctors would recommend such an approach, and I agree that more harm than good would come of it. I have put a stop to that kind of treatment whenever I have encountered it.

Finally, we come to the diet pills, so-called anorexics, which are familiar to most of us because of the frequency with which they are advertised on television. The brands we see on television and in advertising can be purchased over the counter in neighborhood drugstores and contain an ingredient that has been shown to suppress appetite. The prescription-only diet pills contain other, stronger ingredients and are therefore under closer control.

This may be as good a place as any to explain that diet pills don't "take off weight." Their only function is to dampen the appetite. This action often makes it easier for some people to follow a prescribed diet of lesser caloric content, and it's the low-calorie diet that takes the weight off, along with appropriate exercise and behavior modification.

It's only natural to assume that the over-the-counter diet pills are safe to take, since they are available without a doctor's prescription. In certain instances that may be true. However, there are a number of reasons why you should check with your doctor before taking an over-the-counter medication, just as you would before taking a more controlled medication.

First of all, as mild as an over-the-counter appetite suppressant may appear to be, there *is* a systemic effect, and people with diabetes or high blood pressure particularly should be cautioned against taking such medication. Since both conditions may be present, yet be unknown to the patient, indiscriminate use of this type of medication without a preliminary examination may be fraught with danger.

Secondly, the rate at which weight can be safely lost by a particular person is a decision that should be made primarily on the basis of certain medical observations.

Thirdly, some serious side effects have been reported and presumed due to an ingredient common to most over-the-counter appetite suppressants. Your doctor is better able to assess the risk to you such a side effect would pose.

Additionally, over-the-counter medication to suppress appetite is generally considered to be safe and effective for use up to twelve weeks. An interested physician is better able to monitor progress and make adjustments in diet, behavior, and exercise according to the amount of weight loss achieved during those twelve weeks.

Now, what about the prescription-only anorexics? Many of the cautions that apply to over-the-counter appetite suppressants apply equally to their prescription-only counterparts. Of course, with them, a physician is always involved as the prescriber, and so certain scientific principles will govern the choice and control of medication.

The doctor will want to be satisfied that the medication chosen is effective, that it really suppresses appetite. The doctor will want to have seen the results of studies comparing the prescribed medication with a placebo (an inactive substance), showing that the prescribed medication was associated with significantly greater weight loss than was the placebo.

The next matter to interest the physician regarding prescription-only anorexics is their potential for abuse. Formerly, amphetamine was the primary appetite suppressant, but the high degree of abuse and drug dependence that resulted caused U.S. regulatory agencies to withdraw amphetamines from further use as an anorexic. Some prescription-only appetite suppressants resemble amphetamine chemically to a greater or lesser degree. These drugs are classified accordingly as Schedule II, III, or IV drugs. Physicians generally prefer to prescribe drugs that have a lower abuse potential, those classified in Schedule III or IV.

Finally, the incidence and severity of side effects that can be caused by any anorexic influence the physician's choice of appetite suppressant. You may already have read about some disease states, such as diabetes, hypertension, and heart disease, that are often present in overweight persons. Some side effects that occasionally result from some appetite suppressants could cause too much harm to patients with those diseases to warrant their use in most situations. The doctor will be very concious of this kind of danger and will want to be certain that the prescribed anorexic has a relatively low incidence of side effects.

But let's be sure of one thing. You should not interpret any of this to mean that all appetite suppressants are bad. Not at all. Properly chosen, and properly taken, an appetite suppressant can be very helpful in an indicated weight-reduction program. But it should be clear that the choice of whether or not an appetite suppressant is to be used, and which one it should be, is better left to the physician, who is aware of its efficacy, potential for abuse, and safety.

Part Four

MODIFYING YOUR MUSCLES

X

Exercise and Weight Loss

THE NITTY-GRITTY

Not only do most weight-reduction programs include exercise, but the basic rules of health recommended by most authorities do, too. It is generally agreed that exercise, to be effective in weight reduction, should be part of a daily routine. Ideally, it should be performed at the same time each day. Medically, it should be in a form approved by your doctor as being within your physical capacity. From a practical point of view, it should be available without too much trouble or too much interference from inclement weather. The less complicated it is to exercise, the more likely you are to follow your program regularly. The secret of success with exercise is *regularity*.

If your doctor has no objection, you should try to expend about 500 calories a day in physical exercise, or about 3500 calories per week. It has been calculated that expending 500 calories per day in exercising leads to a weight loss of one pound a week.

MYTHS ABOUT MUSCLES

Contrary to the occasional promises contained in advertisements for some weight-reducing salons, it is not possible to pound, massage, roll, or vibrate away fat from a particular part of the body. Dimensions of certain parts of the body are altered by exercise entirely by its effect on the underlying muscles. Thus, an abdomen can be made flatter just by strengthening the abdominal wall muscles by *active* exercise of those muscles.

Further, it is not true that regular exercise increases the appetite. Even greatly increased activity on a regular basis does not increase the appetite of a normal, basically inactive person.

Finally, it must be remembered we are not all cast from the same mold. Heredity largely determines the basic shape of your body, your height, width of pelvic bones, breadth of shoulders, and facial bone structure. You have concealed that basic shape by overlaying it with too much fat. But when you lose excess fat, your basic build will show more clearly. Generally, the fat will come off first in the places it went on first. It is safe to say that your basic build revealed will be more attractive than your overupholstered build ever was. Also, it is not true that a fat face looks better because "the wrinkles are filled in." When weight loss is properly controlled and is not excessive, the "age" lines that may appear on one's face with weight loss are normal and can be more expressive and attractive than a fat double chin.

THE FACTS ABOUT PHYSIQUE

First of all, any exercise, regardless of how simple or how mild, must be within your physical capacity, and your doctor should be consulted for approval of your specific exercise program.

In view of the fact that not everyone can or wants to indulge in a sport that takes a special skill, requires complicated equipment, or is available only through expensive memberships in private clubs, the ideal exercise program almost suggests itself. Walking is the number-one recommendation, by far.

Furthermore, in view of the fact that overweight also manifests itself by creating the well-known "pot," the protruding abdomen, the second ideal kind of muscle-strengthening exercise also suggests itself. Leg-raising and sit-ups that strengthen the abdominal muscles are the top choices in this area.

WALKING: One of the advantages to walking as an exercise is that it can be vigorous or mild to fit individual limitations. It can be made more vigorous by specifying a particular distance within a certain time. It can be made even more vigorous by altering the grade of the route from a slight upslope to the actual climbing of stairs. Finally, it can be modified into its most strenuous forms of running or jumping rope, if the physical condition permits.

A second advantage lies in the fact that the weather rarely makes walking impossible, except in severe storms. Even when such conditions temporarily limit the distance available for walking, one can go back and forth on a shorter route and still accomplish the same result.

Finally, it is possible, if financial conditions permit, to purchase a treadmill type of apparatus on which a very effective program of walking can be followed without leaving the room in which the treadmill is located. It is not necessary to get complicated equipment with a motor-driven belt. The modest upward slant of the walking surface of the treadmill provides all the "work" necessary to make the exercise effective. A stationary bicycle can accomplish similar results if pedal resistance can be adjusted.

STRENGTHENING ABDOMINAL MUSCLES: One advantage of concentrating on strengthening the abdominal muscles is that, as they get firmer, the abdomen looks flatter and you will look slimmer.

A second advantage lies in the fact that these exercises can be done with no special equipment, in the privacy of one's own room or office, and at any time.

Figure 1. Start by lying on your back, with arms extended alongside your head and legs straight and together (see illustration). The toes may be hooked under a chair rung or other furniture to provide an anchor. Bring the arms forward above you and roll forward up to a sitting position as you slide your hands along your legs and grasp your ankles (see illustration). Repeat.

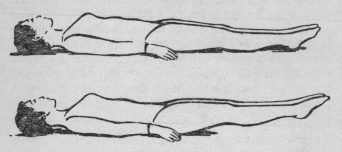

Figure 2. Start by lying on your back, arms down at your sides (see illustration). Keeping your knees stiff, raise your feet four to six inches off the floor and hold this position for four seconds (see illustration). Repeat. Be sure to count out loud while performing the leg-raise so you can't hold your breath and risk causing an internal hernia through the diaphragm.

OTHER ACTIVITIES

Sometimes your daily program will include a special activity that requires you to forgo your usual exercise schedule. Some of those special activities are included in Table 7.

You can see at a glance how many calories you will expend per minute or per hour, as the case may be. This table may help you to keep your exercise program on track.

Table 7

CALORIES EXPENDED DURING VARIOUS PHYSICAL ACTIVITIES

Activities of Short Duration	Cal. per Min.
Making beds	5*
Mopping floors	5*
Sweeping floors	2*
Taking a shower	4
Walking upstairs	20

Activities of Longer Duration	Cal. per Hour
Bicycling	480
Bowling	485
Dancing	240
Golf (if you walk)	330
Jogging	1020
Ping-Pong	290
Routine household chores	120
Sawing wood	415
Shoveling snow	425
Swimming	725
Tennis	420
Walking outdoors	366

*Approximate

THE EXERCISE PLAN

After you have gotten your doctor's advice about how much exercise you should take in accordance with your age and physical condition, plan as follows if your condition is good:

a) Do your abdominal-muscle-strengthening exercises every morning before you dress for the day. The exercises are easier to do without outer clothing to hamper your movements. If you are unaccustomed to these exercises, you may only be able to do each one once at the beginning. Strive to increase the number you can do as you continue your weight-reduction program. Your goal should be to do each exercise five times every morning.

b) Walk briskly for an hour each day. Walk a couple of steps farther down the road when taking the bus. Take your lunch to a park or to the other end of the parking lot instead of eating at your desk. When you are on holiday, don't take your car everywhere. Try walking. Whenever possible, if your doctor has approved, climb the stairs instead of taking the elevator. Walking up a flight of stairs uses up more calories per minute than most sports do, as you see in Table 7. If you have a treadmill or a stationary bicycle, follow the same program.

c) If other activity preempts your regular exercise, try to match the calories usually expended by referring to Table 7 for an exercise you can substitute.

Remember, the secret of success with exercise is regularity.

Part Five

BEHAVING YOURSELF AND LIKING IT

XI

Behavior Modification

As you have probably realized by now, properly programmed weight reduction involves making certain changes in your life-style to form new attitudes, new eating habits, and a proper rest and exercise schedule. The required changes are not all easy, and some are more difficult for one person than for another. The secret of permanent success in weight reduction is to learn the habits that induce the weight loss so well that they remain with you forever. It follows that your weight will remain controlled, too.

One of the ways to help you develop your new habits is to read about them every day. Make it your business to review the following pages each evening until the contents become second nature to you. You may find it much easier to follow your new schedule once you've learned the helpful hints contained in this section.

It's Not What You Do, It's the Way That You Do It

Behavior modification means learning new habits to replace those that have resulted in your overweight. Up to now, you have read about *what* to do—what to eat, what kind of exercise to engage in. Behavior modification is more of *how* to eat, how to arrange your life. Modifying your behavior gives you another outstanding opportunity to make a *positive* approach to reducing your weight. Remember? That's your new creed, the *positive* approach.

What Behavior Modification Does

Diet, exercise, and appetite suppressants, properly applied, will cause some degree of weight loss in almost everyone. But such weight loss usually lasts just for a short time. When the maximum or desired weight loss has been achieved, most patients gradually resume their former habits and weight gain recurs. Behavior modification helps to *prolong* the weight loss, or even to increase it in many cases.

In terms of more *permanent* benefit from a program of weight reduction, *Behavior Modification* is the key!

Does Behavior Modification Work?

You bet it does. If you are really motivated to take weight off, to improve your health—present or future—and to improve your self image, behavior modification adds an important ingredient for success.

Scientific investigations have shown that modifying behavior is most successful when participants in a weight reduction program meet in groups, to reinforce each other's behavior and accomplishments. Many of the commercial weight reduction programs are structured on this premise. However, it has also been shown that the drop-out rate from these commercial programs is often higher than fifty percent, even though the participants have paid rather substantial amounts of money up front to join the program. So group therapy isn't the whole answer by itself.

The investigators have also shown that persons seeking to lose weight are more successful with their behavior modification if they participate in such activity in pairs, rather than alone. In other words, if your spouse—if you have one—will cooperate with your efforts to modify your behavior, your chance of success will be greater. If you are sans spouse, a roommate or close friend will do. All that's required is that the cooperating individual learn the new behavior you will adopt and help you carry it out.

But all of this doesn't mean that if you're alone in your behavior modification activities, you are doomed to failure. Not on your life! Investigators have also known that a book like this one can provide sufficient inspiration to egg you on to your desired goal. And when the physician you've taken into your confidence, and who may be specially interested in you because of your sincere desire to lose weight, provides gentle supervision and encouragement, success lies within reach. I'm doing my best to urge you to grab it.

How You Go About Modifying Your Behavior

First, you must be sure you've picked realistic goals, taking into account your physical condition as defined by your physician, and that you are properly motivated. You must sharpen your awareness of the benefits weight loss will have for you.

You must also determine that you will make every effort to continue the actions I'm going to tell you about that will help to make your weight loss more permanent, even after you no longer have to concentrate so hard on them. Ideally, after you've learned your new habits, they can become so much a part of you that you will scarcely have to think of them. It may not be easy. After all, you've had your bad habits for a long time.

But—and it's a big "but"—don't let yourself be overwhelmed by any of this. Most modification of your behavior can be accomplished as you go along in your weight reduction program, modifying as much as you can handle at a time. It is *not* necessary to do it all at once and it may work out better for you if behavior modification proceeds at *your* pace.

The First Step in Behavior Modification

It is enormously helpful to identify the particular components of your behavior that need modifying. After all, you can't be *all* bad. And it's easier if you can concentrate on the areas that need the most help.

One way to identify those areas is to take a self-assessment test. I've devised such a test to help in the identification. It's time now to take it.

Table 8

SELF-ASSESSMENT TEST

Be as objective as you can about yourself and *circle* the point score of each statement in the test form that applies to you—more than one circle in any subcategory if more than one statement is applicable. By the same token, don't circle anything that doesn't apply to you, even if you leave a subcategory blank.

Add up the points you score in each subcategory, and then the grand total of points for each general category.

Finally, you should compare your point totals with those in the Final Score Table on pages 79–80. Put a big check mark next to the point ranges in each category in which your scores fall. You will see how urgently you need to modify your behavior to help you accomplish and maintain your weight loss, to become a pleasure to behold, and to be a joy forever.

Present Behavior

My eating habits
  I snack:
never	⓪
once or twice a week	①
on hors d'oeuvres and cocktails daily	③
while watching TV nightly	③
at most between-meal opportunities	④
every chance I get	⑤

  I eat out a lot:
business lunches 2 or more times per week	③
restaurant dinners 2 or more times per week	④
social dining out at a friend's home once a week or more	③

Usually when I eat a meal:
I'm the last one finished.	1
I always leave some food on my plate.	1
I finish with the others.	2
I'm the first one finished.	3
I gulp my food.	4
I often take second helpings.	4

The following are true when I eat:
I read or watch TV.	4
I'm at my workplace or in my car.	4
Serving dishes are left on the table.	3
I'm bored, nervous, angry, or excited.	4
none of the above	0

My tastes are as follows:
I eat sweets and/or desserts frequently.	4
I use sugar in my coffee and cereal.	3
I salt most foods.	4
I can eat anything.	3

Eating habits total points_____

My life-style:

I sleep
a good 8 hours every night.	0
6 hours, but I feel refreshed.	1
poorly sometimes.	3
poorly most of the time.	4

I work*
under high tension a full day.	4
at a job I really don't like.	3
and I'm generally satisfied.	2
but I'm happy as a clam.	1

As for hobbies and/or sports,
I'm busy with one or the other most of the time.	1
I don't participate, but I attend games and other events frequently.	2
I do something of the above about once a month.	3
I watch TV or read when I'm not working.	4
I prefer to sit, rather than "do."	5

Life style total points_____

*the wealthy retired can skip this section

My attitudes

Toward my losing weight:

I want to lose weight for important health reasons.	1
I want to lose weight because my appearance is vital to my success.	2
I need to lose weight to fit into last year's clothes/bathing suit.	3
I made a bet I could lose more weight than my husband/wife/friend.	3

Toward my chance of success:

Being overweight runs in my family.	3
Many of my friends are overweight.	3
My spouse is overweight.	4
My children are overweight.	4
They don't think I'm overweight.	4
I'd like to lose weight, but I don't have much hope.	5

Attitude total points_____
Grand Total of all categories_____

If you've scored a Grand Total of less than 14 points, you've made a mistake! There's no way you can be overweight if your behavior is that good. Better go back and take the test again.

If you've scored 14 points or more, turn to the Final Score Table beginning on the next page to see which of your particular behavior problems need modifying. Be sure to put a check mark next to the point range in each category in which your point scores on the Self-assessment Test fall. For instance, if your total point score under *My eating habits* is 15, you would place your check mark on the Final Score Table next to 14 to 20 points under *eating habits* and follow the instructions in that point-range section. Do the same for the other categories.

Table 9

FINAL SCORE TABLE

(The instructions in each section below refer to the Behavior
Modification Nitty-Gritty Table on pages 80–82.)

Under eating habits: if you've scored	
21 points	You're in trouble! You need a complete overhaul of your eating habits. See page 80.
14 to 20 points	You're not much better off. Begin right away to work on all the subcategories in which you circled 4 points or more.
8 to 13 points	Pretty good, but be sure to work on the one or two 4-point subcategory scores.
7 points or less	You're OK. Keep up the good work, but pay some attention to any scores of 3.

Under life-style: if you've scored	
12 or more points	You've got to turn things around right away. Even if it takes some drastic moves, you'll never regret it. See page 82.
8 to 11 points	See if you can't help yourself in the 4-point score subcategories.
5 to 7 points	Not bad, but don't get complacent. It's always possible to improve a little.

Under attitudes: if you've scored	
10 points or more	You don't really understand your problem. Better read about the hazards of overweight again, beginning on page 25.
6 to 9 points	That's a start, but you should develop better reasons to want to lose weight. Remember, motivation is important!

2 to 5 points	You're on track—keep thinking those good thoughts.
1 point	Perfect! The best and most important reason in the world for wanting to lose weight!

What to Do About Your High Scores

The following sections in the Behavior Modification Nitty-Gritty Table tell you what to do to modify the behavior patterns that have helped to cause your overweight. Changing those behavior patterns will help you lose weight and can help to make that weight loss longer lasting. Concentrate on the suggestions for modifying your behavior you checked on the Final Score Table where your point scores from the Self-assessment Test fell.

To help you develop your new habits, read those suggestions over every day. Review them until they become second nature to you. It will take only a few minutes a day to do that. Then follow them to the letter.

When you feel you've *really* made a permanent change in your eating habits, life-style, or attitude, record that fact on the *Record of Your Success* Table on page 92.

Table 10

BEHAVIOR MODIFICATION: THE NITTY-GRITTY TABLE

To change your eating habits for the better:

re: snacking	Delay the snack for 20 to 30 minutes. Set a timer if you can and make a bargain that you'll eat only after the timer goes off. Hunger pangs may last only about 20 minutes. After that you're home free without the calories. Drink a low-calorie soft drink instead of the daily cocktail.

re: eating out	Make up some good excuses and have them ready. Then you can arrive after the meal and still have a good time. Failing that, eat a low-calorie snack *before* you go out to dinner.
re: eating fast	Eat more slowly. Put your fork or spoon down between bites. Chew and swallow your food before picking it up again. You'll feel satisfied sooner in the meal. Try to arrange to have the hot foods served on a hot dish so they won't cool down too much as you eat slowly. Buy or borrow a dish cover—the kind they use in restaurants. Put it over your dinner plate to keep the food warm between bites.
re: eating circumstances	When you eat, make it your *only* activity. Other activities that accompany your eating will just serve as cues to stimulate eating, and you don't need any more of those. Leave no serving dishes on the table to tempt you. Choose a special place to eat to eliminate other areas becoming stimuli for eating. Eliminate all angry and disagreeable talk at the table. High emotions often trigger excess eating.
re: sweet tooth	Remove all displayed tidbits from sight, including candy and nut dishes. Replace eating sweets with low-calorie snacks of carrots and celery. Cross the street rather than pass a bakery or candy/ice cream store.

To modify your life-style:

re: sleeping	Ask your doctor for medical help if you can't get a good night's sleep. It will help you avoid raiding the refrigerator during the night.
re: your work	Start a hobby or arts and crafts project to wind you down from the day's tensions. Reexamine your job and try to find more satisfaction in it than you've managed so far. After all, if you improve your approach to your work, might that not lead to a promotion? Would a short vacation help?

To improve your attitude:

re: losing weight	Bets that you'll lose more weight than someone else, and reducing to fit into last year's clothes, are all right, but be sure you read again about the connection between overweight and illness and mortality. We want you to stick around and enjoy life! Don't let us down.
re: your chance of success	Better regroup your troops. Get your spouse to cooperate and join in your weight loss program, if possible. Try to concentrate less on your overweight friends and favor those who eat less and do more. But, regardless, you can do it all by yourself if you have to. You can succeed!

Don't forget! You should read over the above instructions that apply to you every day until they become second nature.

XII

How to Look Thinner Than You Are

Everyone has two images, a self-image and an image that's projected to the rest of the world. A good part of each of those images consists of one's sense of satisfaction, feeling of accomplishment, degree of success, personal relationships, and other such sociophilosophical ingredients. Another part of each image is strictly visual. My experience in weight reduction tells me that an improved physical appearance can be a quick reward for following the weight-reduction program properly. Quick rewards make good motivation. If you're well motivated, you'll find it easier to follow your weight-reduction program. Let's look at some of the ways you can make yourself look thinner than you are.

First of all, we must deal with you yourself, not your clothes. One way extra fat manifests itself is by creating horizontal lines across your body. Fat on your abdomen makes rolls *across* your body, not up and down. A double chin makes folds *across* your neck, not up and down. The rolls of fat that gather over the kidneys extend *across* your back, not up and down. So horizontal lines suggest excess fat, and therefore horizontal lines should be covered up or counteracted wherever possible if you want to look slimmer. Weight reduction will ultimately remove those horizontal rolls of fat. There are some things you can do in the meantime to lessen their impact on your image.

In the first place, there's your posture. Man or woman, you must learn to stand straighter, sit straighter, and walk more upright. You will then appear taller and you will *be* taller. Even a half inch makes a difference. Standing, sitting, and walking taller add a touch of physical grace, and physical grace is more often a characteristic of slim rather than fat. You will begin to project the image of losing weight even before you actually lose very much. Besides, the effort of standing, sitting, and walking taller adds physical effort to those activities, with the resulting expenditure of more calories than you would ordinarily use up. Make up your mind right now to stand tall, sit tall, and walk tall.

Next, you must pay attention to your hair. That's the one part of your body you can rearrange, if necessary, to create the image of less weight rather than more. In general, hairstyles that emphasize the horizontal line embellish the look of overweight and should be avoided.

For overweight women, this suggests that hair should be done in an upswept style that avoids heavy curls around the neck and shoulders and eliminates a part in the middle of the head. The upswept style adds to the illusion of height and decreases the appearance of width. The hairstyle should not be elaborate, either. The simpler your hairdo can be, the slimmer you will look.

Overweight women who color their hair should avoid loud or brassy colors. Bright henna rinses and straw-colored blond dyes are better saved for leaner days. I also think pitch-black hair is too stark for the average pudgy face. If your hair is one of those colors, I think you should change it. The most flattering tints for the overweight woman's hair are soft browns, honey color, or barely blond. Try one of them. You'll like it.

Men have two opportunities to improve hairstyles: on their heads and on their faces. Overweight men, too, should avoid parting their hair in the middle, because the hair on each side of the part extends horizontally, adding to the overweight look. Ideally, their hair should be parted on the side and brushed back. This adds to the man's height and eliminates the horizontal look. The curly look should be avoided, as well. If a hair dressing will control hair without looking greasy, it should be used. If hair is very curly or kinky and unruly, it should be kept short and shaped close to the head.

Bald men require a somewhat different approach. When the rim of hair is substantial, it can be allowed to grow a little longer and brushed back along the sides. If the rim of hair is very shallow and the hair is thin, it should be kept very short or even shaved off completely, à la Telly Savalas. Under no circumstances should an overweight bald man comb long strings of hair from one side of his head to the other. That's like drawing the horizontal line in neon.

The other opportunity the overweight man with facial hair has to look thinner is presented by the judicious trimming of mustache, beard, or sideburns. It is not possible to discuss all the possible designs and combinations of designs of facial hair that minimize pudginess of face, but the same principles noted above apply. Sideburns cut close to the skin but left heavy enough to be well defined enhance the up-and-down look and narrow the appearance of the face. A mustache that is fairly thin and extends diagonally downward on each side from the midline is better for getting rid of the horizontal look than the heavy, straight-across mustache. A beard that is narrow and extends downward to something of a point adds to the up-and-down look and may partially obscure a double chin.

Whatever the arrangement of scalp or facial hair, it should never be allowed to grow scraggly or become unkempt. Neatness enhances the impression of a good self-image. A good self-image usually improves the image the rest of the world sees. It's worth cultivating.

Clothes also have to be discussed by sex, to a certain extent, and for women may be better left mainly to current fashion magazines. However, there are a few principles both men and women who are overweight should follow. Overweight people should *not* wear tight clothes. The fat lady with the flowered tank top and tight stretch pants and the big-bellied man with the too-small T-shirt and low-cut jeans are, in my opinion, too ludicrous to mention. They seem to be *trying* to look fat, for whatever reason, and are poor examples for those who wish to appear thinner than they are.

Needless to say, most people trying to lose weight can't purchase successive wardrobes to fit as their

Figure 3. *These two figures are exactly the same size.* Notice how the vertical lines of the dress on the right make her look slimmer than the horizontal-striped clothing on the left.

measurements get smaller. However, most people can pick out the few items in their current wardrobes that create a slimmer look and stick with them until their ideal weight is reached. You may find it possible and desirable to purchase some articles of clothing during your weight-loss period that do not depend entirely on your present size, such as a tie (for a man), or (for a woman) a wraparound skirt that adjusts to decreasing measurements. The following suggestions can guide you in choosing the items in your present wardrobe that will make you look slimmer than you are while you grow slimmer than you've been.

In general, overweight people should wear clothes of greater length—longer skirts for women, longer jackets for both men and women—to emphasize that important up-and-down look. The portion of clothing that covers the most overweight part of the body—for instance, hips and thighs, potbelly, or overprominent posterior—should be a dark and preferably solid color. People who are fat all over should wear dark clothes all over—dark suits, dark dresses, dark coats. Large floral patterns and plaids should be avoided at all costs. Up-and-down pinstripes or thin stripes of muted colors enhance the thin look, and judiciously placed darker-colored side panels in women's dresses create the illusion of less suet and more svelte. Many fashion magazines carry helpful hints for choosing dresses that are slimming. They should be consulted for details.

Overweight men should wear suits and jackets with narrow lapels, single-breasted and long enough to completely cover the seat of the pants. They should wear longer-pointed collars and narrow ties. Bow ties with their horizontal look are to be avoided.

Sweaters worn instead of jackets should be cardigan in style to take advantage of the vertical line of closure.

They should be of solid color and big enough that they aren't pulled into those telltale horizontal wrinkles. A cardigan sweater that doesn't button easily across an overweight chest or abdomen should be left unbuttoned completely.

Don't let any monotony of dress during your weight-loss period disturb you. You're much better off looking slimmer each day, however much the same you are, than bursting forth in new but chubby splendor every time the sun comes up.

Have faith. Your time for sartorial splendor is coming.

Part Six

THE SWEET SMELL OF SUCCESS

XIII

The Results

Nothing succeeds like success. Watching your weight go down is the greatest pleasure you can have as you work to get to the lighter side of life.

You or your doctor recorded your weight at the start of your weight-reduction program. Now be sure to weigh yourself on the same day each week, wearing similar clothing each time, and place a dot on the chart in Table 11 to show how many pounds you lost that week. Each week, connect the dots by drawing a line from last week's dot to this week's. Weigh yourself every day if you want to. If you haven't lost in a couple of days, don't worry. Weight is lost in jumps anyway, and a temporary setback may stimulate you to work a little harder.

Recognizing your success with modifying your behavior is also important. When you feel you have accomplished any of the changes in your behavior listed below, write the letter that identifies your new behavior in the box in Table 11 that records *when* you accomplished each change. (The boxes are big enough to hold *two* letters if you are fortunate enough to modify your behavior in less than three months.)

- Ⓐ I have learned to eat more slowly.
- Ⓑ I have substituted non-eating activities in place of snacking.
- Ⓒ I have learned to cope with tempting situations without resorting to increased eating.

Table 11

YOUR PERSONAL WEIGHT LOSS RECORD

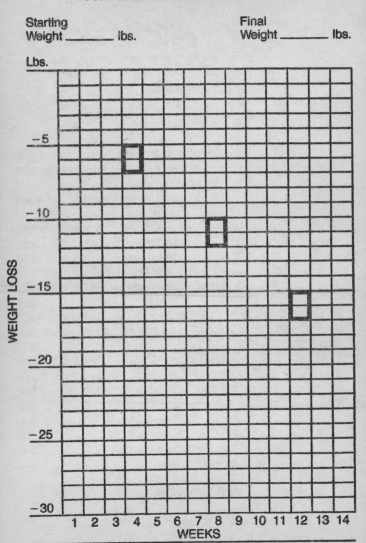

As you connect the dots, you can enjoy the visual evidence of your success, and as you earn the right to place the letters A, B, and C in the special boxes, you can gain confidence in your ability to *maintain* your weight loss.

XIV

Keeping the Weight Off

Now that you have reached your desired weight, it becomes important to maintain it. If you have followed this program, you have learned better eating habits, you have followed a regular program of appropriate exercise, and you have learned how to avoid the temptations that lead to weight gain. You should continue all the good habits you have established and follow the same principles.

Needless to say, you won't have to be as strict with your program to keep the weight off as you had to be to get it off. But you must continue the basics as you learned them right from the beginning. Looking both ways before you step off the curb will help you avoid being hit by a car that time. But you have to look again every time you cross the street to maintain your good record. It's the same with weight loss. You always have to pay attention.

On the following pages you will find lists of foods and some of my favorite recipes that provide fewer calories but still are nourishing. Instead of unnecessarily high-calorie foods, lower-calorie but equally attractive substitutes are suggested. Because they make such beautiful music out of what might otherwise sound like groans of dissatisfaction, I call them my Thin Pan Alley. Follow these suggestions and you have a much better chance of maintaining your weight loss.

THIN PAN ALLEY

The simplest way to eliminate unnecessary calories is by eating comparable foods with a lower calorie count. Of course, the foods should be just as nourishing and filling as the foods you once ate, if possible. The list that follows makes such substitutions more convenient. (A more complete list of the caloric values of standard portions of common American foods appears in the Appendix on pages 120–24.)

But remember! Watch the size of your portions. Stick to the amounts specified in the table that follows and don't take second helpings.

Enjoy your food!

Table 12

THE INSTEAD OFS

Instead of These	Calories	Substitute These	Calories
Salads			
Chef salad with oil dressing, 1 tbsp.	180	Chef salad with dietetic dressing, 1 tbsp.	40
Chef salad with mayonnaise, 1 tbsp.	125	Chef salad with dietetic dressing, 1 tbsp.	40
Chef salad with Roquefort, blue, Russian, French dressing, 1 tbsp.	105	Chef salad with dietetic dressing 1 tbsp.	40
Sandwiches			
Club	375	Bacon and tomato (open)	200
Peanut butter and jelly	275	Egg salad (open)	165
Turkey with gravy, 3 tbsp.	520	Hamburger, lean (open), 3 oz.	200
Snacks			
Chocolate, 1 oz. bar	145	Toasted marshmallows, 4	80
Fudge, 1 oz.	115	Vanilla wafers (dietetic), 2	50
Peanuts (roasted), 1 cup shelled	1375	Grapes, 1 cup	65
Peanuts (salted), 1 oz.	170	Apple, 1	100
Potato chips, 10 med.	115	Pretzels, 10 small sticks	35

Instead of These / Substitute These

Instead of These	Calories	Substitute These	Calories
Soups			
Bean, 1 cup	190	Beef noodle, 1 cup	110
Creamed, 1 cup	210	Chicken noodle, 1 cup	110
Minestrone, 1 cup	105	Beef bouillon, 1 cup	10
Vegetables			
Baked beans, 1 cup	320	Green beans, 1 cup	30
Corn (canned), 1 cup	185	Cauliflower, 1 cup	30
Lima beans, 1 cup	160	Asparagus, 1 cup	30
Peas (canned), 1 cup	145	Asparagus, 12 spears	40
Potatoes			
Fried, 1 cup	480	Baked (2½" diam.)	100
Mashed, 1 cup	245	Boiled (2½" diam.)	100
Succotash, 1 cup	260	Spinach, 1 cup	40
Winter squash, 1 cup	75	Summer squash, 1 cup	30

Based on material from *Are You Really Serious about Losing Weight?*, 13th ed., 1980, © R$_x$ Division, Pennwalt Corporation, with permission.

Instead of These	Calories	Substitute These	Calories
Beverages			
Beer (1 bottle), 12 oz.	175	Liquor (1½ oz.) with soda or water, 8 oz.	120
Chocolate malted milk shake, 8 oz.	500	Lemonade (sweetened), 8 oz.	100
Cocoa (all milk), 8 oz.	235	Cocoa (milk and water), 8 oz.	140
Coffee (with cream and 2 tsp. sugar)	110	Coffee (black with artificial sweetener)	0
Milk (whole), 8 oz.	165	Milk (buttermilk, skim), 8 oz.	80
Orange juice (4 oz.)	50	Consommé, 1 cup	10
Prune juice, 8 oz.	170	Tomato juice, 8 oz.	50
Soft drinks, 8 oz.	105	Diet soft drinks, 8 oz.	1 or 2
Breads			
White bread, 2 slices	126	Gluten bread, 2 slices	70
Danish pastry, 1 small	140	Low-calorie cookies, 2	50
Breakfast foods			
Eggs (scrambled), 2	240	Eggs (boiled, poached)	160
Wheat bran, corn flakes, rice flakes, 1–1¼ cups	110	Puffed rice, puffed wheat, 1 cup	50

Instead of These	Calories	Substitute These	Calories
Butter and Cheese			
Butter on toast	170	Apple butter on toast	90
Butter, 2 pats	100	Margarine, low-calorie	34
Cheese (blue, Cheddar, cream, Swiss), 1 oz.	105	Cheese (cottage, uncreamed), 1 oz.	25

Desserts			
Angel food cake, 2" piece	110	Cantaloupe melon, ½	40
Cheese cake, 2" piece	200	Watermelon, ½" slice (10" diam.)	60
Chocolate cake with icing, 2" piece	525	Sponge cake, 2" piece	120
Cookies, assorted (3" diam.), 1	120	Vanilla wafer (dietetic), 1	25
Cupcake, white icing, 1	230	Plain cupcake, 1	115
Custard (4 oz. cup)	205	Low-calorie cookies	50
Fruit cake, 2" piece	115	Grapes, 1 cup	65
Ice cream, 4 oz.	150	Yogurt (flavored), 4 oz.	60
Pound cake, 1-oz. piece	140	Plums, 2	50
Pudding (flavored), ½ cup	140	Pudding (dietetic, nonfat milk), ½ cup	60
Pies			
Apple, 1 piece	338	A citrus fruit, 1 small	40-50
Blueberry, 1 piece	290	Blueberries (unsweetened), ½ cup	45
Cherry, 1 piece	355	Cherries (whole), ½ cup	40
Custard, 1 piece	280	Banana, 1 small	85
Lemon meringue, 1 piece	305	Flavored gelatin, ½ cup	70
Peach, 1 piece	280	Peach (whole), 1	35
Rhubarb, 1 piece	265	Cantaloupe, ¼	55

Fish and Fowl			
Duck (roasted), 3 oz.	310	Chicken (roasted), 3 oz.	160
Fish sticks, 5 sticks or 4 oz.	200	Swordfish (broiled), 3 oz.	140
Lobster meat, 4 oz., with 2 tbsp. butter	300	Lobster meat, 4 oz., with lemon	95
Ocean perch (fried), 4 oz.	260	Bass, 4 oz.	105
Oysters (fried), 6	400	Oysters (shell w/sauce), 6	100
Tuna (canned), 3 oz.	165	Crabmeat (canned), 3 oz.	80

Instead of These		Substitute These	
	Calories		Calories
Meats			
Bacon, 2 slices	100	Bacon, 1 slice	50
Hamburger (av. fat, broiled), 3 oz.	240	Hamburger (lean, broiled), 3 oz.	145
Loin roast, 3 oz.	290	Pot roast (round), 3 oz.	160
Meat loaf	680	Club steak	320
Pork chop (med.), 3 oz.	340	Veal chop (med.), 3 oz.	185
Pork roast, 3 oz.	310	Veal roast, 3 oz.	230
Pork sausage, 3 oz.	405	Ham (boiled, lean), 3 oz.	200
Porterhouse steak, 3 oz.	250	Club steak, 3 oz.	160
Rib lamb chop (med.), 3 oz.	300	Lamb leg roast (lean only), 3 oz.	160
Rump roast, 3 oz.	290	Rib roast, 3 oz.	200
Swiss steak, 3½ oz.	300	Liver (fried), 2½ oz.	210

MY FAVORITE RECIPES

Taste is such a matter of individual preference that it's impossible to design a dish that will please everyone's palate. My general experience is that, when it comes to low-calorie gourmet dining, chicken and fish lend themselves best as main ingredients. Meats have enough fat in them to make it necessary to keep their preparation simple. Meats that are simply boiled or broiled don't really require special recipes.

The following six recipes for chicken and fish have been gathered gradually over the years from now-forgotten sources. They are not author originals, they are only author favorites whenever it comes time (as it frequently does) to hold back on caloric intake in order to hold the line in the battle of the bulge.

I hope you find them as tasty and useful in your battle as I do.

Breast of Chicken au Limon
Ingredients
   ½ boned and skinned chicken breast per person
   lemon juice   paprika   fresh ground pepper

Directions

Marinate the chicken breasts in lemon juice for a couple of hours. Add paprika and fresh ground pepper. Broil until nicely brown and tender.

Baked Chicken au Limon

Ingredients

3 tablespoons fresh lemon juice
2 tablespoons low-calorie margarine
1 clove garlic, crushed
freshly ground pepper
1 frýing chicken (2½ to 3 pounds), cut into pieces suitable for serving and skinned

Directions

In a bowl, combine lemon juice, margarine, garlic, and pepper. Arrange pieces of chicken in a shallow casserole or baking dish and pour the lemon juice and margarine mixture over them. Cover the casserole/dish and bake at 350°, basting occasionally, until the chicken is tender. This usually takes about 40 minutes. Uncover the casscrole and bake 10 minutes longer to allow the chicken to brown nicely.

Provides 4 servings of approximately 215 calories each.

Filet of Flounder en Foille

Ingredients

1 tablespoon shallot bulbs or green onions
low-calorie margarine
½ pound chopped mushrooms
3 tablespoons dry white wine
1 tablespoon lemon juice
1 tablespoon chopped parsley
4 flounder fillets (approximately 3 ounces each)
freshly ground black pepper

Directions

Sauté the shallot bulbs or green onions in margarine until soft. Add mushrooms and cook for 5 minutes.

Stir in the wine, lemon juice, and parsley and cook until most of the liquid evaporates and the mixture has the consistency of a sauce. Lightly coat 4 pieces of heavy-duty foil with margarine. Place one fillet on each piece of foil, season with pepper, and spoon some mushroom sauce over each fillet. Draw the edges of the foil together and fold them over tightly to seal. Bake at 400° for 20 minutes or until the fish flakes. Serve in the foil.

Provides 4 servings of approximately 250 calories each.

Red Snapper in the Sunset
Ingredients
freshly ground black pepper
2 tablespoons orange juice
1 teaspoon grated orange rind
3 tablespoons low-calorie margarine
1½ pounds red snapper fillets cut into 6 pieces suitable for serving
nutmeg

Directions
Combine pepper, orange juice, rind, and margarine. Place fish fillets in a single layer in a pan lightly coated with margarine and pour the orange juice–margarine mixture over the fish. Sprinkle with nutmeg and bake at 350° for 20 to 30 minutes until lightly browned.

Provides 6 servings of approximately 230 calories each.

Baked Scallops au Vin
Ingredients
1 tablespoon margarine
¼ cup dry white wine
juice of 1 lemon
½ teaspoon thyme
1 pound scallops (bay scallops when in season)

Directions
Heat margarine, wine, lemon, and thyme together. Pour over the rinsed scallops. Marinate for 15 to 20 minutes at room temperature. Bake in 450° oven for 5 to 6 minutes at the most. Do not overcook.

Provides 4 servings of approximately 165 calories each.

Swordfish Supreme
Ingredients
1 pound swordfish (for 2)
lemon juice
freshly ground pepper
paprika

Directions
Marinate the swordfish in lemon juice for about 30 minutes. Add the freshly ground pepper and paprika. Broil on both sides until nicely browned.

Provides 2 servings of approximately 250 calories each.

APPENDIX

This section contains the following items which may be useful in your pursuit of ideal weight:

- A table of common kitchen measurement equivalents
- A desirable-weight chart
- An already calculated 1000-calorie diet
- A table of foods with particularly high sodium content
- A list of America's favorite foods and the caloric values of standard portions.

Table 13

COMMON KITCHEN
MEASUREMENT EQUIVALENTS

Dry Measure
1 pound = 16 ounces = 454 grams
1 ounce = approx. 30 grams
100 grams = approx. 3 ounces

Fluid Measure
4 cups = 2 pints = 1 quart = 32 ounces
1 cup = 8 ounces = 16 tablespoons
¾ cup = 12 tablespoons
⅔ cup = 10 tablespoons plus 2 teaspoons
½ cup = 8 tablespoons
⅓ cup = 5 tablespoons plus 1 teaspoon
¼ cup = 4 tablespoons
1 tablespoon = 3 teaspoons = ½ ounce

It's a good idea to purchase a small scale graduated in ounces and a container for liquids marked off in cups, if you do not already possess these items. They save by-guess-and-by-gosh-sized portions and help you get the most out of your efforts to follow your diet accurately.

Table 14

1983 METROPOLITAN HEIGHT AND WEIGHT TABLES
(based on *1979 Build Study*, Society of Actuaries and Association of Life Insurance Medical Directors of America, 1980)

Height* (feet–inches)	Small Frame** (pounds)	Medium Frame** (pounds)	Large Frame** (pounds)
5' 2"	128–134	131–141	138–150
5' 3"	130–136	133–143	140–153
5' 4"	132–138	135–145	142–156
5' 5"	134–140	137–148	144–160
5' 6"	136–142	139–151	146–164
5' 7"	138–145	142–154	149–168
5' 8"	140–148	145–157	152–172
5' 9"	142–151	148–160	155–176
5'10"	144–154	151–163	158–180
5'11"	146–157	154–166	161–184
6' 0"	149–160	157–170	164–188
6' 1"	152–164	160–174	168–192
6' 2"	155–168	164–178	172–197
6' 3"	158–172	167–182	176–202
6' 4"	162–176	171–187	181–207

Men 25-59 Years

Women 25-59 Years

Height* (feet— inches)	Small Frame** (pounds)	Medium Frame** (pounds)	Large Frame** (pounds)
4'10"	102–111	109–121	118–131
4'11"	103–113	111–123	120–134
5' 0"	104–115	113–126	122–137
5' 1"	106–118	115–129	125–140
5' 2"	108–121	118–132	128–143
5' 3"	111–124	121–135	131–147
5' 4"	114–127	124–138	134–151
5' 5"	117–130	127–141	137–155
5' 6"	120–133	130–144	140–159
5' 7"	123–136	133–147	143–163
5' 8"	126–139	136–150	146–167
5' 9"	129–142	139–153	149–170
5'10"	132–145	142–156	152–173
5'11"	135–148	145–159	155–176
6' 0"	138–151	148–162	158–179

*In indoor clothing weighing 5 lbs, shoes with 1" heels
**Generally, a man has a small frame if he wears a hat smaller than size 7, a medium frame if size 7 to 7½, large if over 7½. A woman has a small frame if her glove size is below 6, medium if 6 to 7, large if over 7.
Reprinted from *The Apothecary*, February, 1981 with permission of the Metropolitan Life Insurance Company.

1000-CALORIE DIET

After you've used this diet for a while, I think you'll agree it wears well. The accent is on variety. You choose what you want to eat. In many instances, you can actually choose how much. Most important of all, you probably won't go away from the table hungry . . . which is the best way in the world to stick to a diet and lose weight.

Although you don't have to figure out all the caloric values for yourself, you do have to choose a menu that follows the rules. Be sure your doctor has approved this 1000-calorie diet formula for you before you start it.

Incidentally, this particular version of a 1000-calorie diet is one I've developed over the years from standard diets that have originated from various authoritative sources. My modifications are based solely on my own experience with patient acceptance of such prescribed diets. It's a good version of a 1000-calorie diet, but if your doctor has one you like better, by all means use it.

1000-Calorie Diet for Adults

Each day, choose the principal foods you like. Select your favorite meat, fish, or poultry from the lean, medium lean, and medium fat groups beginning on page 114. Each group must be chosen with equal frequency. If you prefer to limit your selection to the lean and medium varieties only, you may increase the size of your portion from medium to large. The calorie value will be the same, but you will get more protein and less fat. Choose your preferred vegetables next, then round out your slimming diet by picking the list of optional foods (I, II, or III) that suits your fancy that particular day (see Table 15, p. 110). You will find your daily diet plan conforms pretty much to the following schema:

What you eat	How much to eat	Number of calories
Skimmed milk	2 cups	170
Cottage cheese	⅔ cup	200
Egg	1 medium	75
Meat, fish, or poultry	1 medium portion	280
12½-calorie vegetables	4 portions of ½ cup each	50
Optional foods	As specified in I, II, or III below	225
		Total 1000

Suggested Menu Plans*

With (Category I foods added)	With (Category II foods added)	With (Category III foods added)
Breakfast		
½ cup orange juice	½ grapefruit	1 orange
1 egg, boiled or poached	⅔ cup cottage cheese	⅔ cup oatmeal
1 thin slice bread	2 pieces melba toast	1 cup skimmed milk
Beverage	Beverage	1 egg, boiled or poached
		Beverage
Lunch		
4 oz. dietetic tuna fish†	Sandwich (2 thin slices bread, 1 hard-cooked egg with celery, tomato, and lettuce)	Celery and radishes
Lettuce, tomato, celery		⅔ cup cottage cheese
1 cup skimmed milk		½ cup carrots
	1 cup skimmed milk	6 asparagus tips
		Beverage
Dinner		
½ cup tomato juice	6 oz. hamburger, broiled	6 oz. broiled flounder
6 oz. roast veal	½ cup Brussels sprouts	Salad—lettuce, variety like escarole, endive with celery, green pepper
½ cup beets	Cabbage salad	
½ cup grated carrot salad	Beverage	
1 pear		1 cup strawberries (fresh or dietetic, low-calorie syrup)
Beverage		Beverage
Bedtime		
1 cup skimmed milk	1 cup skimmed milk	1 cup skimmed milk

*Average approximate values: protein, 100 g; carbohydrate, 94 g; fat, 30 g (27%).
†4 oz. dietetic tuna fish (170 calories) substituted for ⅔ cup cottage cheese (200 calories).

Table 15

OPTIONAL FOODS FOR 1000-CALORIE DIET

Category*	No. Portions	Food	Calories	Total Calories	See Page
I	1	50-calorie bread	50		111
	2	50-calorie fruits	100	225	112
	3	25-calorie vegetables	75		112
II	2	25-calorie breads	50		111
	2	50-calorie breads	100	225	111
	1	50-calorie fruit	50		112
	1	25-calorie vegetable	25		113
III	1	100-calorie cereal	100		111
	2	25-calorie fruits	50	225	112
	1	50-calorie fruit	50		112
	1	25-calorie vegetable	25		113

*Add all the foods in the category you've chosen to your diet that day. Do not add foods from different categories.

Table 16

Calorie Value of Bread, Cereals and Related Products

Bread (including white, rye, whole wheat, cracked wheat, protein, etc.)	1 thin slice	50
Melba toast	1 piece	15
Rusk, Holland	1 rusk	50
Ry-Krisp	1 piece	25
Cereals, cooked (after cooking)	⅔ cup	100
Cereals, dry flaked (corn flakes, Rice Krispies, Wheaties, Rice Toasties)	⅔ cup	100
Shredded Wheat	1 large biscuit	100
Crackers and Cookies		
Arrowroot biscuit	1 biscuit	25
Chocolate wafer	1 wafer	50
Fig bars (Newtons)	1 bar	50
Gingersnaps	1 snap	50
Graham Crackers	1 cracker 2½"	50
Macaroons	1 macaroon	50
Oreo Sandwich	1 wafer	50
Oysterettes	6 crackers	25
Peanut Butter	1 cookie	50
Pretzels	5 small sticks	25
	1 large	50
Ritz	3 wafers	50
Shortbread (Lorna Doone)	1 cracker	50
Social Tea biscuits	1 biscuit	25
Soda cracker	1 cracker	25
Vanilla wafers	1 wafer	5

Calorie Value of Common Fruits

One standard portion is 1/2 cup. Syrup-packed fruits, or fruits with added sugar, are not listed.

25-Calorie Fruits
  Cantaloupe (1/4 medium)
  Cranberries
  Honeydew melon*
  Lemon
  Strawberries
  Watermelon

50-Calorie Fruits
  Apple juice
  Applesauce
  Apricots, canned, waterpacked, fresh (3 medium)
  Blackberries
  Blueberries
  Cherries, sour
  Fruit cocktail, fresh or waterpacked
  Grapefruit, canned, fresh (1/2 small)
  Grapefruit juice, fresh or canned
  Grapefruit and orange juice blend
  Grapes
  Guava (1 medium)
  Honeydew melon (1 two-inch wedge)*
  Loganberries
  Nectarine (1 medium)
  Orange (1 medium)
  Orange juice, fresh or canned
  Peaches
  Pear (1 medium)
  Pineapple, fresh or canned, waterpacked
  Plums (1 medium)
  Raspberries, fresh
  Tangerine

---

*Honeydew melon is included in both the 25- and 50-calorie groups, depending on how it is served. One-half cup is given a 25-calorie value, while a 2-inch wedge is given a calorie value of 50.

APPENDIX

Calorie Values of Common Vegetables

No butter or fats in cooking, or mayonnaise or French dressing on salad vegetables. *One standard portion is ½ cup.* In the menus, vegetables or fruits may be substituted for others with the same calorie count.

12½-Calorie-Value Vegetables
Asparagus, fresh and canned stalks (6 stalks)
Beans, string*
Beet greens
Broccoli
Cabbage
Cauliflower
Celery
Chard
Cucumber
Dandelion greens
Endive
Escarole
Lettuce
Mushrooms
Parsley
Peppers
Pickles, unsweetened, sour, dill or sweetened
  with saccharin
Pimientos
Radishes
Rhubarb
Sauerkraut
Spinach
Squash, summer
Turnip greens
Watercress

25-Calorie-Value Vegetables

Beets, fresh and canned	Scallions (6 small)
Brussels sprouts	Tomato juice
Carrots	Tomatoes, fresh and canned
Eggplant	Turnips
Leeks	

---
*Well-filled string beans have a 25-calorie value.

Calorie Value of Dairy Foods

Cheese, cottage (including "creamed" cottage, pot cheese, farmer cheese) all others	1/3 cup	100
(including cream cheese)	1 oz.	100
Egg	1 medium	75
Milk: skimmed-milk buttermilk	1 cup	85
buttermilk	1 cup	92
evaporated, unsweetened	1 oz.	45
skimmed, fluid	1 cup	89
skimmed, dried powder	1 tbsp.	25
whole, fluid	1 cup	170
whole, dried powder	1 tbsp.	50

Calorie Value of Meat, Fish, Poultry, Shellfish

Lean
   Small: 4 oz. portion—100
   Med.: 6 oz. portion—150
   Large: 8 oz. portion—200
   Bass, striped
   Brains, all varieties
   Chicken, breast only
   Clams (1 dozen)
   Cod
   Crabmeat
   Finnan haddie
   Flounder
   Haddock
   Kidney, pork and sheep
   Lobster
   Oysters
   Pike
   Scallops
   Shrimp
   Sturgeon
   Sweetbreads, calf and lamb
   Trout, brook only
   Weakfish

Medium Lean
  Small: 4 oz. portion—170
  Med.: 6 oz. portion—250
  Large: 8 oz. portion—340
  Bluefish
  Butterfish
  Chicken (other than breast)
  Eels
  Halibut
  Herring
  Kidney, beef
  Liver
  Mackerel
  Rabbit
  Salmon, canned
  Sardine in tomato sauce
  Shad
  Shad roe
  Swordfish
  Trout, lake
  Tuna fish, fresh
  Turkey (light meat only)
  Veal, all cuts, average
  Whitefish

Medium Fat
  Small: 4 oz. portion—260
  Med.: 6 oz. portion—400
  Large: 8 oz. portion—520
  Beef, all cuts, average
  Bologna sausage
  Frankfurters (2, 3, or 4)
  Herring, pickled
  Bismarck, kippered
  Lamb, all cuts, average
  Liver sausage
  Liverwurst
  Salmon, fresh
  Sardines, canned in oil
  Tongue
  Tuna fish, canned
  Turkey (except light meat)

Food Items Without a Calorie Value

Beverages
  Coffee without added sugar, cream or milk
  Postum without added sugar, cream or milk
  Tea without added sugar, cream or milk
  Carbonated water
  Mineral water, natural or artificial
  Non-calorie, flavored carbonated beverages
  Sugar substitutes
    Saccharin
    Sucaryl improved

Seasoning Agents
  Celery salt
  Chives as seasoning
  Dill
  Monosodium glutamate
  Horseradish
  Lemon, juice, sections or slices*
  Mustard
  Pepper, all varieties
  Salt
  Sauces, prepared such as Worcestershire, A-1
  Tabasco
  Spices
  Vinegar, cider, wine or artificial
  Garlic*

Relishes
  Bread and butter pickles*
  Cucumber pickles*
  Dill pickles*
  India relish*
  Pickled onions*
  Sour pickles*

*These items all contain a few calories, but for practical purposes, when used in customary amounts as seasoning or relishes or as a thickening agent, the calories are insignificant.

Adapted from Joliffe, N., in *Clinical Nutrition*, 2nd ed., 1962, pp. 960-973, copyright 1952, 1957, 1963 by Simon & Schuster, Inc., with permission.

WHEN SALT RESTRICTION HAS BEEN PRESCRIBED

This table will come in handy when you have to know right up front which foods to avoid. If your doctor says, "No salt," don't be foolish. Avoid these foods like the plague.

Table 17

FOODS WITH A PARTICULARLY HIGH SODIUM CONTENT

Vegetables
Tomato juice
Sauerkraut
Pickles
Vegetables prepared
  in brine

Fruits
Olives

Soups
Bouillon
Clear soups without fat
Consommé

Meats and Meat Substitutes
Bacon
Cold cuts
Bologna
Chipped beef
Corned beef
Frankfurters
Hamburger and bun
Ham
Salt pork
Sausage
Any smoked meat
Low-fat cottage cheese
Processed cheese
  Cheese spreads
  Roquefort
  Camembert
  Gorgonzola
  Cheese pizza

Fish
Anchovies
Caviar
Cod, salted and dried
Herring
Sardines

Snacks
Crackers with salt topping
Cheese curls
Potato chips
Pretzels
Salted nuts
Salted popcorn

Bread
Bread and rolls with salt topping
Some brands of English muffins

Miscellaneous
Chili con carne with beans

Desserts and Beverages
Some sugar-free sodas
Chocolate pudding
Apple pie

Seasonings
Catsup
Celery salt
Chili sauce
Cooking wine
Garlic salt
Meat extracts
Meat sauces
Onion salt
Prepared mustard
Relishes
Tenderizers
Worcestershire sauce

AMERICA'S FAVORITE FOODS

I hope I've convinced you that dieting doesn't have to be dull.

You've lost weight. You follow a program of regular exercise. You've learned to prefer lower-calorie foods to the fattening foods you once ate.

The following pages contain lists of popular foods with their caloric values by categories for ready reference. You may find this information handy to have with you when you travel or visit. Eating a weight-controlling diet can be very satisfying.

Besides, knowing that you have your caloric intake under control will make your meals more enjoyable. It's really quite easy to *eat* and *smile* at the same time!

Table 18

CALORIC VALUES OF STANDARD PORTIONS OF COMMON AMERICAN FOODS

Cereals, Grains, Breads	Amount	Calories
Bran flakes	1 cup	105
Corn flakes	1 cup	100
Cracked wheat bread	1 slice	65
Doughnut, plain	1	125
Farina, oatmeal	1 cup	105
French bread	1 slice	50
Shredded wheat	1 biscuit	100
Raisin bread	1 slice	70
Roll, hard	1	155
Roll, soft	1	200
Rice, cooked, white	1 cup	225
Rye bread	1 slice	60
Spaghetti	1 cup cooked	155
Spaghetti/meat balls	1 cup	330
Spaghetti/cheese	1 cup	260
Noodles, cooked	1 cup	200
Macaroni/cheese	1 cup	430
White bread	1 slice	70
Whole wheat bread	1 slice	70

Vegetables		
Asparagus, cooked	4 spears	10
Beans, canned, baked	1 cup	300
Beans, green, cooked	1 cup	30
Beets, cooked	1 cup	55
Broccoli, cooked	1 cup	40
Cabbage, cooked	1 cup	40
Carrots, cooked	1 cup	45
Carrots, raw	1 medium	25
Cauliflower, cooked	1 cup	25
Coleslaw	2/3 cup	70
Corn, cooked	2/3 cup	115
Celery	1 cup	15
Cucumber	1 medium	30
Lettuce	1/4 head	15
Mushrooms, canned	1 cup	40

	Amount	Calories
Onions, cooked	1 cup	60
Onion, raw	1 medium	40
Peas, cooked	½ cup	60
Potato, sweet, baked	1	155
Potato, white, baked	1	105
Radishes, raw	4	5
Spinach, cooked	1 cup	40
Turnips, cooked	1 cup	35

Dairy Products

	Amount	Calories
Butter	1 tbsp.	100
Buttermilk	1 cup	245
Cheese, blue, Swiss	1 oz.	105
Cheese, cottage	4 oz.	120
Cheese, Cheddar	1 oz.	115
Cheese spread	1 oz.	80
Egg, boiled	1	80
Egg, scrambled, fried	1	110
Ice cream	½ cup	130
Milk, whole	1 cup	160
Milk, skim	1 cup	90
Cream, heavy	1 tbsp.	55
Cream, half and half	1 tbsp.	30
Yogurt, plain	1 cup	135

Meats and Poultry

	Amount	Calories
Bacon, broiled	2 strips	90
Beef hamburger	3 oz.	245
Beef pot roast	3 oz.	245
Beef roast, lean	3 oz.	210
Boiled ham, sliced	3 oz.	200
Bologna	3 slices	120
Chicken, turkey, fried	4 oz.	190
Chicken, turkey, roasted	4 oz.	180
Lamb chop, lean	4 oz.	200
Lamb leg, lean	5 oz.	260
Liver, fried	2 oz.	130
Liverwurst	1 slice	80
Frankfurter (cooked)	1	142
Pork chop	1	260
Pork, ham	3 oz.	310

	Amount	Calories
Pork spareribs	3 ribs	250
Salami	1 oz.	130
Steak, broiled	3 oz.	250
Veal cutlet	3 oz.	185

Seafood

Clams	3 oz.	65
Crabmeat, canned	3 oz.	85
Codfish, fresh	4 oz.	150
Flounder	3 oz.	200
Halibut	3 oz.	150
Salmon, canned	3 oz.	120
Sardines, drained	3 oz.	180
Shrimp, shelled	3 oz.	100
Tuna, canned	3 oz.	170

Soups

Beef noodle	1 cup	70
Chicken noodle	1 cup	65
Chicken with rice	1 cup	40
Consommé	1 cup	30
Clam chowder, Manhattan	1 cup	80
Clam chowder, New England	1 cup	210
Minestrone	1 cup	105
Onion	¾ cup	50
Tomato	1 cup	90
Tomato, cream of	1 cup	175
Vegetable	1 cup	80

Beverages

Carbonated, sweet	6 oz.	60
Carbonated, artif. sweetener	6 oz.	2-12
Coffee, tea, black	1 cup	0
Coffee, tea w/milk and sugar	1 cup	35
Club soda	8 oz.	0
Beer	12 oz.	150
Daiquiri	3½ oz.	200
Manhattan, sweet	3½ oz.	164
Rum, vodka, whiskey	1½ oz.	115
Wine, dry	3½ oz.	84
Wine, sweet	3½ oz.	140

	Amount	Calories
Sweets, Candies, Desserts		
Angel food cake	1" slice	165
Brownies	1	95
Caramels	1 oz.	115
Chocolate bar	1 oz.	145
Chocolate cake, iced	2" slice	450
Chocolate syrup, thin	1 oz.	90
Cookies	1 medium	50
Cornstarch pudding	½ cup	190
Gelatin dessert	1 cup	140
Hard candy	1 oz.	110
Honey	1 tbsp.	65
Jams, jellies	1 tbsp.	55
Marshmallows	1 oz.	90
Pie, apple, cherry, peach	1 slice	350
Pie, lemon meringue	1 slice	305
Popsicle	3 oz.	70
Pound cake, plain	½" slice	140
Sherbet	1 cup	260
Sponge cake, plain	1" slice	235
Sugars	1 tbsp.	40
Oils, Dressings		
Diet margarine	1 tbsp.	50
Margarine	1 tbsp.	100
Vegetable cooking oil	1 tbsp.	125
French, Italian dressing	1 tbsp.	65
Mayonnaise dressing	1 tbsp.	100
Russian dressing	1 tbsp.	50
Catsup	1 tbsp.	15
Fruits and Fruit Products		
Apple	1 large	70
Applesauce, unsweetened	½ cup	50
Apple juice, unsweetened	1 cup	130
Apricots, canned	½ cup	110
Avocado	½	185
Banana	1 medium	100
Cantaloupe, honeydew	½	60
Fruit cocktail	½ cup	100
Grapefruit	½	45

	Amount	Calories
Grapefruit juice	1 cup	110
Grapes, green	1 cup	65
Lemon, lime	1 medium	20
Olives, green	2	15
Orange	1 medium	65
Orange juice	1 cup	110
Peach	1 medium	35
Pear	1 medium	100
Pineapple, canned	2 slices	90
Plums	3 medium	75
Prunes, cooked	4 oz.	150
Raspberries	1 cup	70
Strawberries	1 cup	55
Tomato	1 medium	40
Tomato juice	1 cup	45
Watermelon	slice 4″ × 8″	115

Snacks

	Amount	Calories
Dill pickle	1 medium	10
Gherkin, sweet	1 medium	20
Mixed nuts	1 cup	785
Peanut butter	1 tbsp.	95
Dry roasted nuts	1 cup	840
Potato chips	10	115
Pretzels (3-ring)	1	25
Soda crackers	3	50

Based on U.S. Dept. Agriculture Sources. *Nutritive Value of Foods*. Home and Garden Bulletin No. 72. U.S. Dept. of Agriculture. Rev. January 1971.